A Christian Life Without Father God

Leanne Goff

DEDICATION

First I want to give thanks to my Father God who has loved me and believed in me even when I didn't believe in Him. He has always been a Father to this fatherless one. He is the best Dad in the whole world, and I want everyone to know about my amazing Dad.

Secondly, I want to dedicate this, my first book, to the love of my life, Ray Goff. You have been a Mordecai in my life and without you I truly do not know where I'd be today. You were the first person to demonstrate unconditional love to me. Your grace and patience toward me over the years of our marriage, particularly the first ten, carried me through many times when I wanted to give up. You are the best husband, greatest dad, and most awesome grandfather anyone could ever ask for. I look forward to many more years together.

AKNOWLEDGMENTS

I want to thank Leif Hetland, my spiritual father, for teaching me to See Through Heaven's Eyes! For demonstrating to me what it looks like to walk out, *"and I have made Your name known to them, and will make it known, so that the love with which You loved Me may be in them, and I in them."* (John 17:26)

I would like to also thank Jessie Hansen, Sonia Silva, and Helen Trotter for their assistance in contributing to the editing and finalization of this book. You've all been such a blessing to my life. The best is yet to come!

ENDORSEMENTS

A deep, quiet, and life-changing transition is taking place in our world today. It is happening across the cultures of the world, is not driven by the media, nor can it be stopped or sidelined. It will succeed! We really do not know God, as He desires to be known, until we know Him as Father. When we begin to see the centrality of this truth in the Bible, we hold a new book in our hands.

Because of testimonies of those like Leanne Goff and those she presents in this splendid book; the Father revelation of God is increasing in intensity in both breadth and depth. Leanne walks us through the most painful seasons of her life. She came out not only a presentation of what it means to call God "Father," but she has also come into a powerful alignment with the Kingdom of God...the Family Business. She has become her message, pointing to a path made clear, on how to become a son or daughter of God. Thanks, Leanne!

A testimony is irrefutable, sustainable, and beyond human logic. This book will aid you in understanding the "where-to-from-here" issue for those who are finding God as Father. Welcome to the eternal future and the Kingdom: Family of God!

Jack Taylor
President, Dimensions Ministries
Melbourne, FL

This is a wonderful book to read. As with many orphans around the world, the difficulties of life without knowing a father are reflected in the different stages of Leanne's life. Her strength and determination will inspire many.

I have personally been a witness to the growth of Leanne, Mom, as we call her in Cuba. Several years ago, she brought us her passion for the nations. Her love as a mother to us has been an important part of the transformation of our lives.

A Christian Life without Father God makes us reflect on ourselves, while challenging us to find the God who loves and completely transforms hearts.

Josue' Santiago
Director, Kingdom in Action Family
Mantanzas, Cuba

Leanne's first book is a testimony of perseverance, hope, and the reminder of the love of our Heavenly Father. Hers is the story of a wonderful husband, spiritual Dads, and a call to the nations. Everyone will connect to the exciting, winding road that's her life story, and in reading will be encouraged to chase his or her promises and inheritance.

Steve Hale
Senior Pastor, Bethel Atlanta
Atlanta, GA

We live in one of the most fatherless generations in the history of the world. If your heart is broken and you feel rejected, abandoned, or you simply struggle to feel loved, Leanne Goff's book, *A Christian Life Without Father God,* is a must read. This book will cut a trail through the jungle of broken relationships, betrayals and abuse, while paving a path to passion in your heart that you never thought was possible.

I highly recommend this book and believe that many people

will be released from the prison camp of a loveless master into the arms of their loving Father.

Kris Vallotton
Leader, Bethel Church,
Redding, CA
Co-Founder of Bethel School of Supernatural Ministry
Author of nine books including:
The Supernatural Ways of Royalty and *Spirit Wars*

In 2003 I personally witnessed a permanent transformation of a woman I had known for over a decade. She had always been passionate and productive in the things of God, but something changed on the floor of Toronto Christian Fellowship. Leanne Goff encountered the Father she had always longed for. She went down an orphan and arose a daughter. All of us who know her have experienced the benefits of that encounter.

Leanne has been a ministry partner, friend, and now is a part of my family. I can attest to the truth of this book. Read it and rejoice. But more than that, let it awaken within you a hunger for deeper encounters with the same Father who wants to transform you, as well.

Dave Olson
Senior Pastor, Heartland Church
Ankeny, IA

Meeting Leanne Goff was for me meeting a living testimony of the power that lies in finding our true identity as sons and daughters of our perfect Father. In this book, *A Christian Life Without Father God*, she tells her story in a way that is easy to read, but gives plenty of opportunities to be impacted and transformed. You will find biblical insights, along with a true story that is impossible not to be touched by. We need more books like this!

> ***Egil Elling Ellingsen***
> Pastor, IMI Kirken
> Stavanger, Norway

As you prepare to read this book, I want you to know what you read will not be theory, opinion, or dry facts, but the experiences of a woman of God who has lived out what she is writing.

While we worked together in the ministry of Teen Challenge for several years, it is what God has done in her and through her since leaving us that is truly amazing. She is someone who lives out godly character and integrity in all that she does.

God has called Leanne to the nations and given her favor everywhere she goes. Leanne's life challenges me to strive to be a better husband, father, and leader. Read this book with a hungry heart. It can and will change your life.

> ***Roger L. Helle***
> Former Executive Director
> Teen Challenge of the Mid-South
> Chattanooga, TN
> Author of *My War Beyond Vietnam*

In this wonderful book, *A Christian Life without Father God,* Leanne Goff invites us into a journey of knowing and experiencing God as *our* Father. With courage and humility, she shares her life's stories interwoven with the powerful revelations of Father's Love that radically transformed her life, as well as the lives of many others.

As I read through the pages, I was reminded of when Joseph finally revealed himself to his brothers who sold him into Egypt. Joseph forgave his brothers. Joseph became a blessing, not just to his family, but to the nations, as well. The life and journey of Leanne with our Father reflects this. I recommend her book to all who are seeking deeper intimacy with God, our Papa.

Paul Yadao
Lead Pastor, Destiny Ministries International
Los Banos, Philippines
Author of *The Mark*

In my personal and ministry interaction with Leanne Goff, I've come to know her as a person of *passion* and *purpose*. We are working with her, Leif Hetland, and Global Mission Awareness in targeting the largest unreached people groups of Pakistan. In her book, *A Christian Life Without Father God*, Leanne traces her spiritual pilgrimage from a young person to a mature minister of God. She highlights her profound spiritual experiences, and has formed her life into an awesome, fruitful ministry.

Dr. Howard Foltz
Founder and President Accelerating
International Missions Strategies (AIMS)
Colorado Springs, CO

"A Father of the fatherless, a defender of widows,
Is God in His Holy Habitation."
~ Psalm 68:5 ~

CONTENTS

Leanne Goff

FOREWORD

BY LEIF HETLAND

This book can and will change lives! *A Christian Life Without Father God* is an invitation for spiritual orphans to find their way home. The disease and tragedy of Father deficiency is causing more deaths than any other disease in our lives and society.

When I write a foreword for a book, I look for two things. First, is this a message that will change lives? Secondly, has the author become the message they are writing about?

Leanne Goff is a spiritual daughter, my former Personal Assistant and Executive Administrator. Over the years, I have seen, and continue to see, Leanne carry a message of the Father's love leading her as a daughter of freedom, fulfillment, and acceptance. *"I will not leave you as orphans. I will come to you."* (John 14:18)

The pages in this book are filled with passion for a passionate Father, that wants all His spiritual orphans to finally come home. You are a beautiful son or daughter that Father God wants to express His love to, and then send you forth to give that love away to others.

I have watched Leanne learn the language of love that is being communicated all over the world. I have watched her in the darkness of Pakistan, amongst the poor in Africa, mothering an army of world changers in Cuba, releasing the Kingdom of God in the Philippines, and expressing the unending love of a wonderful Father across America. She travels with the language of love, bringing transformation to lives and nations.

The Apostle Paul said, *"For if you were to have countless tutors in Christ, yet you would not have many fathers, for in Christ Jesus I became your father through the gospel."* (I Corinthians 4:15) It is with tremendous gratitude and joy I am honored to father a compassionate, competent, and caring spiritual daughter that lives a life well loved.

The foundation of Spiritual Inheritance in the Kingdom of God is found in these pages. A double portion "anointing" is available for anyone that will allow Holy Spirit to lead him or her home.

The Father is waiting! Are you coming?

Leif Hetland
President, Global Mission Awareness
Author of seven books including:
Seeing Through Heaven's Eyes

INTRODUCTION

As I look back through the unfinished book of my life, I can see where the enemy of our souls has attempted to take me out numerous times. As with all of us, he has attempted to prevent me from fulfilling the purpose and *Designed Destiny* my Father God created me to fulfill. Years ago, during my family's mission training with Youth With A Mission, I heard Winkie Pratney make a statement in regard to Proverbs 6:26:

> *"For on account of a harlot one is reduced to a loaf of bread, And an adulteress hunts for the precious life."*

Winkie said that those who have a specific assignment on their lives, the enemy will attempt to do whatever it takes to keep them from fulfilling that assignment. He said that the "precious lives" are the *cream of the crop*. By the world's standards I am a nobody. But in the heart and eyes of my Father God, I am very special; I am one of the *cream of the crop*.

I so agree with my spiritual father, Leif Hetland, when he says, *"Not that I am so qualified, but I am so willing"* to see my assignment completed.

A Year Of Testing

> *"The refining pot is for silver and the furnace for gold, But the LORD tests hearts."*
>
> (Proverbs 17:3)

The year 2011 was a year of testing for me. It wasn't a test of faith, or even my character, but a test of my heart. One day in January 2011 while I was in prayer, God spoke very clearly to me. I was asking Him what 2011 held for me. He said, *"My daughter, 2011 will be a year of testing for you. I'm going to test your heart regarding love...how much do you love me? How much do you love your husband? Your children? Your spiritual family? Your neighbor?"* I'm sure there will be many who will read this book that will find that to be true of their own lives; that they have been in a season of testing.

We go through the tests in life that will qualify us (or disqualify us) to reign as kings and queens representing the Kingdom of our God. Esther's identity was a daughter. What she did was a queen. Daughter was her alignment. Queen was her assignment. Esther, as well as Joseph, Daniel, David, and Nehemiah went through the process of testing that qualified them to reign and to rule within royal communities.

Jesus' forty days in the wilderness was the test of Sonship. I have journeyed through the testing of Sonship to qualify to steward the inheritance given to me by my Father God.

PROLOGUE

The Christmas movie, Elf, is one of my all-time favorites. Every time I watch this movie there are scenes where I laugh hysterically as if watching it for the first time. For instance, ...

❄ *"Have you seen these toilets? They're GINORMOUS!"*

❄ *"We elves try to stick to the four main food groups: candy, candy canes, candy corn, and syrup."*

❄ *"Does someone need a hug?"* when he encounters the raccoon who appears to be discouraged and wandering.

❄ or, Buddy's infamous twelve-second long belch after drinking a 2-liter bottle of coke.

Elf, better known as Buddy, is about one of Santa's elves that lives at the North Pole and learns of his true identity as a human. As Elf grows up he begins to realize that something is just not right. He's not like all the other elves. Buddy is about three feet taller than everyone else. Half his body hangs over the foot of his little bed. His ears aren't pointy like the others at the North Pole. And Elf's abilities to make toys as good and as fast as the other elves is severely lacking.

Finally, Papa Elf sees the great discouragement upon Buddy and sits down to tell Buddy the pain-staking news that he's really not an elf, and he's really not his father. Papa Elf tells Buddy the story of how he came to be at the North Pole. Papa Elf reveals that Buddy was born to Walter Hobbs and Susan Wells. Buddy was given up for adoption.

Buddy grew up his entire life in a world that was not real. The father that raised him was not really his dad. This devastated Buddy and threw him into a state of confusion and disillusionment.

Buddy, with the blessings of Papa Elf, goes to New York City to look for his biological father. When Buddy finds his father, Walter, he doesn't want anything to do with Buddy. In fact, at one point, Walter tells Buddy to get out of his life. All Buddy wanted to do was spend time with his dad and they get to know each other— hold hands, snuggle, go ice skating, eat a batch of tollhouse cookies as fast as they could, make snow angels for two hours, and eat sugar plums—what all kids dream of doing with their dads, right?

Elf's story does have a wonderful ending. Of course, it does, it's a Christmas movie. But in most real-life situations today, this is not how it turns out.

I believe many of us can relate to Buddy. I know I can. I grew up in a world that many times seemed unreal. I felt awkward, out-of-place, a misfit. The older I grew, the more I knew things just didn't line up in life, at least in my life.

In this book, I will share my life, my stories, my hurts and pain, my shortcomings, my failures, and my insecurities. Don't despair; I will also share my victories, triumphs, and breakthroughs, as well as brief messages that Father has given me along the way, many during what we call *The Dark Night of the Soul*.

But what I want to communicate more than anything is how

God was with me through every circumstance, rejection, disappointment, testing, failure, and trial. Even when I thought, *"God where are you? Why have you left me? Why is this happening to me?"* He was with me every minute of every day. *"He **never** left me, nor forsook me"* (See Hebrews 13:5). And He will always be with you, too! He has been a Father to this Fatherless one.

– Leanne Goff

Leanne Goff

ONE

MY DESIGNED DESTINY

The Spirit Himself testifies with our spirit,
that we are the children of God.
~ ROMANS 8:16 ~

When I Grow Up

I was raised in a large Baptist Church just outside of New Orleans, Louisiana. Ever since I was a little girl, all I ever wanted was to be a missionary. I can remember sitting on the front pew of our large church thinking, "When I grow up I want to be a missionary." I didn't know anything else but that. Missionaries would come to our church and speak. They would show their mission work through a slide presentation with their carousel projectors. They would talk about their work in the country they were ministering in and use their clickers saying, (click) "Here we are doing this...." and "Here we are (click) doing that", etc. etc. I think of how far we've come today with multi-media presentations including sounds, graphics, smoke machines, etc. during mission trip report presentations.

Ever since I was a little girl, all I ever wanted was to be a missionary.

I would sit on the pew and be enthralled with the lives of those missionaries and their work in various countries. I would always say, "Wow, that is so cool. I want to do that." It was never a dream of mine

21

to be a teacher, a lawyer, or a doctor, as many would aspire to. Ever since I was a little girl, all I wanted to be was a missionary. I wanted to travel to other countries telling people about Jesus and His saving power.

Even when my mom and stepfather were not believers, my mom worked very hard to make sure my brothers and I were in church as much as possible. My mom worked long hours for an airline, but she'd manage to either find a ride for us on Sunday mornings to church, or she would bring us herself. I'm so thankful that my mom gave her life to Jesus in the early seventies, and lived her life as a prayer warrior up until the day she received her upgrade to heaven.

I grew up in the church. I was very involved in our youth group as much as I could be. The church I went to was First Baptist Church in Kenner, Louisiana, just outside of New Orleans. I was in the youth choir. I was also part of a musical team called The New Revival. I was in Youth For Christ in high school. I went to weekly prayer meetings and Bible studies. I would even go out with teams witnessing in the French Quarter of New Orleans. Bob Harrington's ministry is one I specifically remember working with in the Quarter. Bob Harrington was known, at that time, as The Chaplain of Bourbon Street.

In 1972, our youth group went to Dallas, TX for Explo '72. It was a grand event where thousands of young people from across the United States gathered for one week. During the mornings, we were in workshops and seminars learning how to evangelize and lead people to Christ. In the afternoon, we went out to the streets invading Dallas with the Good News of Jesus, leading many to Christ. In the evenings, we were gathered in Dallas' largest stadium for explosive worship and hearing from speakers such as Billy Graham, Andrae Crouch, Paul and Jan Crouch, and many others.

When I turned seventeen I began to steer away from church. I began hitting the bars and going, what we called in New Orleans at that time, jooking. My all-girl high school was on a platoon system. I went to school 12:30 pm to 6:00 pm. Immediately after school I'd head to my part-time job selling shoes at an exclusive department store in a nearby mall. I did very well in my job, many times making the "top sales" for the month. As soon as I got off at 9:00 pm, I'd head out to the bars. I did more than just drink. Though I never did any hard drugs, marijuana was a favorite of mine.

Drugs and alcohol will numb the pain, but it's God's love that will take it away.

I remember times when I would get so drunk I'd end up at home never knowing how I got there. I realize now that I was attempting to numb the pain that had built up in my life over the years. I was also filled with so much anger. I heard someone say a few years ago, "Drugs and alcohol will numb the pain, but it's God's love that will take it away." So many people attempt to numb the pain in their lives through drugs and alcohol, while never succeeding. It is only the love of our wonderful Papa God that can bring healing, restoration, and freedom to a soul bound up with hurt and wounding. I wish I had had this revelation years ago.

Even when I was out partying and going from bar to bar, there was always something in me that wanted more of God. There was a longing in my heart to know Him in a deeper way than what I had been taught. As I said, I always had a strong desire in my heart to be a missionary.

As I grew older, I particularly had a drawing to the Latin culture. There were no Hispanics in my family line. For that matter, I was around very few Hispanics growing up. But I loved the Spanish language. My heart would flutter when I was in a store and would hear Spanish being spoken down the aisle. God was setting me up for something I hardly knew of at that time.

My Partner For Life

I've been married for forty-three years now to the one God knew I needed in my life. I have the most amazing husband. He has always been supportive of what Father has called me to do in fulfilling my assignment and destiny.

Ray and I met in a bar—Bullwinkle's Tavern. I wasn't quite eighteen at the time, so I used a fake ID to get into the bars. I remember one night when I was at the Rising Sun and the police raided it. Wow, I was shaking in my boots, though I do not remember having boots on. With police officers all over the place, and German Shepherd guard dogs sniffing out the bar for drugs, paraphernalia, etc., I found myself praying that I would get out of that place without being caught.

Normally one's ID was checked before entering a bar. Now the police were checking our ID's before they would let us out of the bar. To make matters worse, my ID had my picture, but the rest of the information was one of my best friend's, Cassidy. It had her name, birthdate, etc. A bigger problem—Cassidy was in the bar with me. We would enter the bar within minutes of each other so the guy at the door checking ID's would be thrown off. Oddly, it always worked.

We had to think quick and come up with a plan so that I would not be caught with a fake ID. I did make it out with no problems. You would have thought I learned my lesson, but no way. I continued to go to the bars night after night.

Ray had long hair to the middle of his back and it was some of the most beautiful hair I had ever seen. It wasn't long and stringy. It was thick and well kept. In fact, today at sixty-six years old, there are so many men envious of Ray's head-full of hair, though it's no longer brown, but full of gray. I was drawn to Ray's hair, his long side burns, and Fu Manchu mustache.

I remember seeing Ray using the pay phone in the mall where I worked and hearing God say, "That is the man you will marry." This came as a shock and surprise to me. I didn't even know this man, but God knew I needed someone like Ray in my life. Even though it would be two years before Ray would give his life to Jesus, Ray showed me unconditional love. I had never experienced that kind of love before.

"That is the man you will marry."

During the first ten years of our marriage, Ray endured a lot of excess baggage that I brought into our marriage. Honestly, he had every reason to say, "I'm out of here." or "You're out of here." But he didn't, and I'm so thankful for that. He just continued to love me while God was healing and restoring me.

Ray and I began dating in December 1973 and were married October 18, 1974. I wish I could say it was perfect love that brought Ray and I together. But in that time of my life, I had no clue what perfect love looked like. In fact, I don't think I knew what normal love looked like. All I know is I was looking to be needed, loved, and accepted. I had so many gaping wounds in my heart.

My Own Little Family

Amid all my frailties and insecurities, I really desired to be a good wife and mother. When our first child was born April 29, 1977, I was thrilled. During my pregnancy, I was working for Tulane University Medical Center in the Department of OB/GYN/Oncology. I loved my job, because other than missions, I was also drawn to the medical field.

Through ultrasounds I was told that I was going to have a boy. This made perfect sense to me seeing that I am the only girl of five, smack dab in the middle of the line-up, and my mom was the only girl of six. So, I just naturally expected a boy. The odds of having a girl were very slim. But God had another plan and I'm so glad He did.

Elizabeth Leigh Goff was a beautiful baby. Beth filled Ray and my hearts to overflowing. She was also a very good baby. She began sleeping through the night when she was just six weeks old. Beth was as bald as a bowling ball for many months. Even though we had her ears pierced within a few weeks of birth and we would dress her in pink, people would continuously stop us in a store or restaurant saying, "Oh, he's so cute." or "What a cute baby boy." It would make me so mad. I wanted to say, "Do you need glasses or something?". But instead I would respond, "Yes, *she* is, isn't *she*?"

Two and one half years later we received our boy, and, oh my, what a boy! Jeffrey Paul Goff was born to us on October 16, 1979. Even though Beth was the apple of her daddy's eye, Jeffrey filled that place in Ray's heart for having a son. I have thoroughly enjoyed the unique personalities of my daughter and son. Beth...ALL girl. Jeff...ALL boy. I wouldn't have wanted it any other way. I'm so proud of my children. Today they are both living their lives for God and expanding His Kingdom throughout the world. God has given them amazing partners and children that are complimenting their marriages.

Hurt People Will Hurt People

Though I was a very good mother over all, I not only carried a lot of excess baggage into my marriage, but my family, as well. No one is ever really prepared for the adventure called parenting. One can take as many parenting classes as possible, but life will throw curve balls your way that will catch you off guard. When you couple the challenges of parenting with love deficits in one's life, like mine, this can make

No one is ever really prepared for the adventure called parenting.

room for inflicting hurt and pain on others. I truly don't believe most of us know what we're doing. But nonetheless, we do it. The statement is true...hurt people will hurt people.

For instance, I never would have laid an unrighteous hand on either of my children. Granted, when they needed to be disciplined and when that warranted a spanking, that would be given, but never harsh treatment or beatings. But there was one thing I did that brought my heart to a near screeching stop one day.

Beth was about five years old. I had just folded a load of clothes and was putting them away. I walked down the hallway of our house towards Beth's room. As I approached her room, she was sitting on the floor with her back toward the doorway playing with

27

her doll, also named Beth. When Jeffrey was born and we brought him home from the hospital, we gave Beth her new baby doll. This way mommy had her new baby and Beth had hers.

When I walked to the doorway of Beth's room, I witnessed her holding her doll by the arm and shaking her saying, "Stop it. Stop it. Don't do that." I couldn't believe it. I realized Beth was acting out exactly what I would do to her whenever I wanted her to obey, or she did something wrong like spill her milk or walk away from me in the grocery store. I was beside myself. I couldn't believe what I had taught my daughter. I walked into her room crying and took her in my arms holding her so tight asking God to forgive me. I knew in my pain and hurt I was inflicting pain and hurt on my little girl. I vowed I would never treat her, or Jeffrey, that way again. I'm thankful to say I never did.

Even though I had been radically saved a few years before this incident, I still had a lot of healing that needed to be done in my heart, as well as a great deal of forgiving.

TWO

FROM THE PEW TO THE NATIONS

For all who are being led by the Spirit of God, these are sons of God.
~ ROMANS 8:14 ~

Snatched From The Grips Of Hell

As I previously mentioned, I was very involved in church and church activities growing up. I had memorized the Four Spiritual Laws, as well as the Roman Road. During those times these two well-known methods were used in witnessing to someone and bringing them to Jesus. I soon became aware that I knew the Word of God, but I did not know the God of the Word. That all changed in September 1976.

I soon became aware that I knew the Word of God, but I did not know the God of the Word.

Our pastor decided to hold his own revival services at our church. Pastor Ron was a wonderful pastor, but more than that he was a dynamic evangelist. One night of the revival services the church was packed with about one thousand people. I hung on to every word that came from Pastor Ron's lips. Ray and I were seated towards the back of the church. I distinctly remember where we were sitting and what I was wearing like it was yesterday. I was totally engaged.

At the end of Pastor Ron's message, he did what most Baptist pastors did back then when they gave an invitation to receive Jesus as Lord and Savior. He said, "Every head bowed, every eye closed, and nobody looking around." So, I did what I had done for many years...bowed my head, closed my eyes, and did not look around. Suddenly I heard God speak to me very clearly. He said, "Leanne, you know all about Me, but you don't know Me. You're on the road to hell." I couldn't believe what I was hearing, but I knew this was truth. All my religious works had gotten me nowhere but lost. Crying, I jumped out of my seat, politely moved my way to the end of the row, and began my journey up the long aisle to the front of the church.

When I arrived at the front and crying profoundly, Pastor Ron came over to me and asked me what was wrong. I said, "Brother Ron, I'm lost. I'm going to hell." Brother Ron would have never been one to try and change my mind. Right then and there I repented of my sins, asked Jesus to come into my heart and be my Savior and Lord. This is something I had done with many others over the years, but I never remembered doing this myself. I would say I worked my way into religion, not relationship. The following Sunday night I was gloriously baptized in water, and a few days later I found out I was pregnant with our first child. I believe there was something special that took place with my child and me as I was baptized with her in my womb.

After that experience, I wanted to tell every person I encountered about my Jesus. I witnessed to everyone. I would have witnessed my newfound relationship to a street pole if it had breath. I fell madly in love with Jesus and wanted everyone to experience what I had experienced.

The Journey Begins

There was a man in our church who had his own ministry called Good News In Action. His name was Leo Humphrey and Leo was not your typical minister. He was different in every way possible.

Leo didn't like wearing suits and ties, which were commonly worn back then by pastors and ministers. Most times one would find Leo in a pair of jeans and a leather vest. Leo was always hugging and loving on everyone around him, which I was not accustomed to.

One thing about Leo that caught my attention more than anything was the fact that he was bringing mission teams into Central America, primarily Honduras and El Salvador, during the height of the Civil War there. When I would hear him speak about his trips and his experiences in Central America, my heart would race. I wanted to do that, but had no clue how it could happen. This awesome man of God had no idea who little ol' me was.

One Sunday morning after church I saw Leo standing out on the walkway. I decided to take my first step toward my dream of being a missionary. I walked up to Leo and introduced myself and said, "I want to go to Central America with you." To my surprise, Leo gave me his phone number and said to give him a call. Well, that's all it took. I called Leo that very next week. Low and behold, he was taking another team back to Honduras in just a few weeks and Ray and I were invited to join him. I was beside myself with excitement.

Ray and I had a few hurdles to jump over to see us make this trip. A big one was the money to pay for the trip. We did not have the money saved, but where there's a will, there is surely a way. We decided to sell a lot of our furniture. We set it out on our front lawn and had a huge sale. Within a matter of a couple of weeks, we had all the money to pay for our trip from the proceeds of our furniture sales. God even went beyond the point of provision.

Within a matter of a couple of weeks, we had all the money to pay for our trip.

I was a real estate agent at the time. Within weeks of our return from Honduras, I had some amazing real estate transactions go through that allowed us to buy all new furniture to replace what we had sold.

A second huge hurdle was getting our passports. I had one as a child, but it had long expired. With my mom working for the airlines, as children we traveled internationally quite a bit during my growing up years. Ray had never had a passport. Basically, we both needed to start from scratch.

Mind you, this was spring 1982 and acquiring a passport was a much longer process then than now. These days one can have their passport in hand within a couple of days. Back then it could take weeks. But we didn't have weeks, so we went to praying.

We decided to drive downtown to the local New Orleans passport agency. We had our applications, photos, money, and birth certificates in hand. We were called to the window and the woman began to look over our paper work. She asked me, "Are you related to Billy Crawley?" I said, "Yes, ma'am. He's my brother." She then said, "Oh Billy used to date my daughter. I really like that boy. I tell you what, I'm going to put a rush on this for you." Ray and I were about to jump out of our skins. We would have

Where God guides... He provides!

our passports in hand in more than enough time to make the trip. Where God guides...He always provides!

The last two details were Ray getting the time off from work to go, and someone staying with the kids, which all worked out with no glitches at all.

It was Easter week and we were off for our first mission trip. I could hardly believe it. After twenty-six years, I was finally stepping into my dream...being a missionary, and I was going with my husband. What more could I ask for?

A lot of people thought Ray and I were crazy. We were going to Central America containing countries with a tremendous amount of unrest. But we were not afraid one bit. We knew God had set this up for us.

It was an amazing trip. We spent a good portion of our time in the main plaza in Tegucigalpa surrounded by throngs of people day and night. We had a mini portable sound system that was strapped to a team member's back. We took turns preaching the Gospel message, following with an invitation for those who wanted to receive Jesus to come forward. They would be led in a prayer of salvation, and then the rest of the team, working with those from a local church, would talk and pray with the newborn believers.

We also went to an orphanage with Easter candy and treats that we had brought for the children. There was a little girl in that orphanage named Christiana that stole Ray's and my hearts. We were so attracted to her that we attempted to adopt her. But sadly, to say, it didn't work out. But another opportunity to adopt a baby would present itself a couple of years later.

Leo preached in the church we were working with on that trip. I loved hearing Leo preach. Leo loved Jesus with all his heart, and everyone he encountered knew it. Leo was one of the coolest people I had ever met. Leo went home to be with Jesus in April 2006. Those present at his funeral told story after story of how Leo had impacted their lives either introducing them to Jesus or stirring their hearts for missions. Leo witnessed to every person he met...each would hear about Jesus' love for them and His plan of salvation before Leo left their presence.

On Easter Sunday morning, we were heading up to a mountain for a sunrise service. We were going through the revolving door of the Hotel Mayan to get into the truck we were going to ride in when suddenly, we heard machine gun fire. We just kept going around in the revolving door back into the hotel.

I remember on other trips there were times machine gun fire would go off in the market and we'd hit the ground for covering. Another time we were in San Salvador, El Salvador and bombs were going off in the mountains. The glass louver windows of the apartment we were staying in would rattle at every explosion. The guerillas had blown up the Shell gas station sign across the street from where we were staying, as well as the movie theatre, to get their point across, attempting to bring fear on the people. But the people of Honduras and El Salvador were so open to the Good News we were bringing them. We saw thousands saved and I loved every minute of it. It is said that in 2012 thirty percent of El Salvador's population are evangelical believers.

The Mission Virus

While on our trip we missed our children greatly and couldn't wait to see them again. By the end of the week of our first trip, Ray

Ray and I were infected with the mission virus.

and I knew we had been infected with the mission virus. We knew we were not called to the typical American lifestyle, which is to work to get money to buy food to eat and then sleep just to get up the next morning and do it all over again. I have always known I was created to disciple nations. Starting from that trip years ago, I wanted to be known on this earth for inheriting nations for His glory as a daughter of Papa God.

Ray and I knew we needed to do something regarding what we had just experienced. For weeks after we were home, we would go through our pictures, once we had them developed, and just cry and cry. We could see every face as if the person was right in front of us, and smell every smell as if it encircled us.

But Ray had concerns. He was the breadwinner of the family and wondered how all this would work out. He had a wife and two small children. He had a very good, secure job as a Weigh Master licensed by the United States government at a grain elevator along the Mississippi River. He also felt we needed some sort of training before we jumped straight into a country in the middle of a war zone as missionaries. At the time the only organization we knew of that trained families for the mission field were the Southern Baptists. We felt that option was not for us.

Eventually, Ray became a Jonah. He began to run from our calling to the nations. I couldn't blame him. It was a huge step.

I continued to travel with Leo a few more times to Honduras over the next couple of years. I was not going to change Ray's mind. I knew it would have to be between him and God.

A couple of years later, Ray and I went back to Honduras together, his second trip. By the end of the trip he was miserable. He knew in his heart what we were destined to do, but had trouble reasoning it out in his mind. I find many Christians in that exact same situation these days.

The economy was becoming very shaky in 1984, and Ray's secure job was becoming not so secure anymore. By the end of the trip, Ray was so moved in his heart that he couldn't sleep the last night. He paced the floor in our hotel room the entire night. One week after our return home, Ray received his pink slip. He had been laid off from his secure job. At that point he told God, "You've taken away my secure job. I know you'll take care of my wife and kids. Now we just need some training."

A Spiritual Boot Camp

Through another amazing set of circumstances, we were introduced to Youth With A Mission (YWAM). YWAM had a mission base in New Orleans and Father God had put us in the direct course of a couple of their base staff. Ray had me invite them over for dinner, and by the end of the night they had arranged for us to visit one of their primary bases in Lindale, Texas. Within a couple of weeks, we all drove over to YWAM Lindale, TX to check it out.

By September 1984 all four of us were going through YWAM's Discipleship Training School (DTS) preparing for, as I reasoned, the mission field. Ray and I became YWAM-ers, and Beth and Jeffrey, were WeeWAM-ers ☺.

We spent two and one-half years with YWAM between Lindale, TX, New Orleans, LA and Guatemala, Central America. During our time with YWAM Guatemala, we came across a baby its mother didn't want. We began going through the process of adopting her. On the morning we were to go pick up the new addition to our family, our attorney received a phone call saying that the mother had decided to give the baby away to someone else. Our hearts sank at the news, but we trusted God knew best.

If you are familiar with YWAM at all, then you know that this amazing ministry, that has literally impacted hundreds of thousands of lives, can bring out the best and the worst in an individual. Living in dorm-style quarters and sharing houses with one to two other families, can make or break you. A YWAM DTS (Discipleship Training School) consists of five months of training— three in a classroom, and two on the field called the outreach phase.

When we joined YWAM, I thought we were going to be trained for the mission field, and though that was surely a part of it, Father God had other plans for me specifically.

I had a deep-rooted seed of father wounding planted in my soul from my childhood. It manifested in bitterness, hatred, anger, and resentment, which needed to be dug out before I could move forward with my life. I loved Jesus and wanted to travel the world telling others about the Good News of Jesus. But Father God knew good and well that I was a very broken woman who needed a lot of healing. I thank God that He put YWAM staff in my life. That was a huge part of initiating the healing and breakthroughs I desperately needed.

One such person was my DTS small group leader, Margie. One Thursday night, after four days of teaching on the Father Heart of God by Doug Easterday, Margie stuck with me for two and one-half hours. I had learned that forgiveness is a decision of my will, and what the outcome could be if I chose not to forgive. At the top of my list was my biological father. Honestly, I DID NOT want to forgive this man. Everything in me was screaming No, don't do it! Margie coached me through. With strong emotions and tears, I made the decision to forgive my father. I cannot begin to tell you the immense relief that followed that decision. I felt as if a ton of bricks had been taken off my shoulders. I began the process of freedom from the effects of twenty-six years of fatherlessness.

During our time with YWAM we also ministered in various cities throughout Mexico. We loved our days with YWAM and anytime we run across a YWAM'er, there's always a deep connection among us. We are grateful for YWAM and their history of impacting nations with the Kingdom of God throughout the many years they've been in existence.

THREE

RECEIVING A BAPTISM OF LOVE

A father of the Fatherless, and a judge for the widows,
is God in his holy habitation.
~ PSALMS 68:5 ~

Teen Challenge

Ray and I spent ten amazing years working with the worldwide ministry Teen Challenge. Many those years were spent under the leadership of Roger and Shirley Helle. We are immensely grateful to Roger and Shirley. They are two of the finest examples of leadership one could ever hope for. Roger and Shirley were with Teen Challenge for thirty-nine years. The centers that Roger and Shirley have overseen have the longest tenure of staff of any Teen Challenge Center in our entire nation.

Teen Challenge has approximately two hundred and fifty centers in the United States. It is primarily a live-in ministry where men and women, chained to life-controlling issues, go to be set free. We began our season of ministry with Teen Challenge in Colfax, IA and Omaha, NE. These centers were two of just a handful of co-ed centers across the country. Ray and I were Evangelism Supervisors. Our responsibilities consisted of taking the students on local outreaches to the downtown streets of Des Moines, as well as rock concerts, prison ministry, and other local outreaches. Also, each student had the opportunity to go on a two-week mission trip to Mexico. For many these trips brought a life-changing dynamic to them.

Our last six years with Teen Challenge was in Chattanooga, TN. This center was a men's program for eighteen years. Ray and I relocated to Teen Challenge Chattanooga specifically to launch a women's program. I was the Women's Director and Ray became the Vice-President of the overall ministry.

A Transformational Breakthrough

In June 2002, we were offered the opportunity to move back to Mexico and work with another ministry. We resigned our positions with Teen Challenge and headed south, a move we later regretted. But God! had a plan that would totally redirect the course of my life.

Things did not go as we thought in Mexico and our stint was short lived. After five months, we moved back to the states, to Iowa. I was devastated. I did not want to be back in the states, though I love my country, much less Iowa. I spiraled down into a state of depression, eventually on anti-depressants, something I never would have previously condoned. I was a wreck and nobody knew what to do with me. I lived this way for months, giving up on anything and everything.

Prior to our move to Mexico, my son-in-law would tell me about this revival in Toronto, Canada. I had been to the Brownsville Revival many times, but had no desire to go to Toronto. However, one day after our move to Iowa, I threw myself on our living room floor and cried out to God. I told Him, "Something has to change in my life.

I know you did not create me to live this way. I don't care anymore about my reputation, my ministry, my credentials, or any titles. I lay them all down before you." Something began to shift in that moment.

I soon found out our church was taking their first team to the revival in Toronto known as <u>The Father's Blessing</u>. I was one of the first to sign up. I was a desperate woman. A few months later we headed to Toronto. Prior to the trip, I remember telling my pastor and friend, Dave Olson, "I know Jesus as not only my savior, but my friend. I am very close to Him. But I still have a hard time with God as my Father. I know He is Father, but *my* Father?"

I knew this had a lot to do with my biological father being totally detached throughout my entire life, and, even though I had this knowledge, it was still part of my problem. On my own I couldn't overcome the feelings that there was any way God could be *my* Father. Orphans can relate to this feeling of knowing the problem, but being helpless to fix it.

My biological father never wanted to have anything to do with me, though he was obviously a significant part of me being created. I believe that biological fathers are to reflect what Father God looks like to their children. So, since my biological father was absent throughout my entire life, I lived with the reasoning that Father God was also absent in my life. God created me, but really didn't want to be with me or be involved in my life.

My view of God was—He tolerated me, but didn't celebrate me. Many times, if I needed something or wanted something from Father God, I would ask my brother, Jesus, to ask Him because I knew He'd do it for him. In my mind this is the ultimate of an orphan mentality.

As soon as I walked into the church in Toronto, I sensed a love that I had NEVER known before. I was so desperate, but so expectant! The first service began and our team was seated in the very back of this huge room of approximately four thousand people from all around the world.

At one point during worship, John Arnott asked for the large group from Mexico to raise their hands. To my delight, this group was seated very close to us. John then asked the entire group to come forward. Then I heard John say, "Anyone who speaks Spanish….". Well that's all I needed. I went forward to be prayed for, as well. God had set me up! See, I thought they were going to pray for those that spoke Spanish, too. How silly, huh? But what John said was, "Anyone who speaks Spanish, would you come up and help us pray for these brothers and sisters from Mexico?"

I found myself up front with all these dark-skinned, black-haired Hispanics, with my eyes closed and in position to be prayed for. It's been said by what happened next, in my desperation, I stole the birthright. Someone, a nobody, on their ministry team came along and just barely touched me and prayed, "More Lord". Well that was it! I landed on the floor and began to wail. I cried and cried for two and one-half hours. During this entire time, I felt the love of my Father, like I had never felt before, flow in and through my being, repeatedly. I was stuck to the floor not being able to move. I was caught up into a love experience with Father God that transformed my life.

When I got up off the floor, my life had been drastically

impacted. I had been baptized in His perfect love, what I call my Baptism of Love. It wasn't a touch, or a change; it was a transformation that has radically altered my life and ministry since. Many family and friends who have known me through the years are a witness to this transformation.

At that point, God became my Dad. He's the best Dad in the whole world and I know that I can go to Him at any time with anything. He spoke to me as I got up off the floor, "Leanne, you've been a Woman of God, a woman of integrity, and a successful minister with a heart after Me. But I don't want a Woman of God anymore. My desire is to have a little girl who knows she has a big Daddy". So now, that's my identity—a little girl with a BIG Daddy, who loves me, is pleased with me, delights in me, and finds me extraordinarily valuable! He doesn't tolerate me—He celebrates me! I'm no longer fatherless!

Receiving Nations As Sons And Daughters

Before I received my Baptism of Love, I worked for nations. Now as a daughter, I receive nations. I've been to twenty-three nations, and have lived in two of those nations. In Mexico alone, we have lived in three cities. The work that we've done in those nations was very good. But I now know there's a greater way. I believe that Esther saved a nation in a day as a daughter, not as a queen. I believe that Joseph received a nation as a son, not as Pharaoh's assistant. Daniel influenced a nation from his identity as a son, not a Jew.

Do you realize all of these individuals were orphans? We don't know how Esther's parents died, but she was left as an orphan, and became a daughter to Mordecai (See Esther 2: 7 & 15). Joseph was sold by his brothers and became an orphan, but as a son became "a father" to Pharaoh (See Genesis 45:8). Daniel was taken from his parents and thrown into one of the most heathenish cultures of all time, but he knew who he was and Whose he was.

In March 2006, Ministry In Action, or MIA (the ministry I was President of at the time), hosted a pastor's conference in Cuba. It was MIA's first conference in Cuba, and a powerful, foundational event. That conference would be the launching pad for much of what we're doing in Cuba today. Those pastors and church leaders who were present didn't have the books, manuals, DVD's and CD's available to them that we have at a finger's touch. We have since provided many resources and tools that are allowing the church in Cuba to grow stronger from a Kingdom perspective.

On the third night of the conference I was laying on the floor during worship. I had been to many nations, living in *"Ask Me for the nations and they shall be yours."* two of them, but there was something about Cuba that had captured my heart. As I laid on the floor in God's presence, I said to Him, "Father, as you gave Heidi Baker Mozambique, I'm asking You for Cuba." (See Psalm 2:7 & 8) He said, "Daughter, it's yours. Take it!" At that moment, I reached my hand toward heaven and took Cuba and put it in my heart. Cuba's been there ever since.

The theme scripture for MIA was Psalm 2:8, "Ask of Me, and I will surely give the nations as Your inheritance, And the very ends of the earth as Your possession." We see this scripture displayed at mission conferences, or posted on banners in our churches. But we have failed to recognize what verse 7 says, "Son, ask..." I believe as we embrace the truth and live from our identity as sons and daughters of a loving Father, we will receive more nations to disciple for His Kingdom and Glory.

People have asked me how I did that. I tell them it was supernatural. I just did it from a position of daughtership. Many times, I'll tell them, "A brown cow eats green grass and gives us white milk. I do not try to figure out the process. I just drink the milk." By the way, I love milk, especially with hot tollhouse chocolate chip cookies.

In the LGM and GMA spiritual family, we do not work for nations any longer. We receive them as sons and daughters. This way is so much easier, and much more fun, too. No laboring or striving...just receiving.

My Introduction To Leif Hetland

I had heard the name Leif Hetland, but really didn't know who he was. In June 2006, I joined a Global Awakening team to China. On this trip one of Global Awakening's team leaders, Tom Jones, asked me if I knew who Leif Hetland was. I told him I had heard of him, but didn't know him.

Just a few months later, in October 2006, I met Leif Hetland at a Global Awakening conference in Mechanicsburg, Pennsylvania. We were both members of Global Awakening's Apostolic Network (ANGA), and were both scheduled to be licensed at their annual Voice of the Apostles' (VOA) Conference. It was our like-hearts for Cuba, as well as the nations, that connected us. At that conference, we talked about Cuba and our experiences in this amazing nation. We kept in contact with each other after we left the conference, even doing a joint trip to Cuba with our mission teams in June 2007.

When I met Leif I had my own ministry, Ministry In Action. MIA was all about hosting ministry teams to various nations. MIA's home base was in Ankeny, IA, in association with Heartland Assembly Church. I had an amazing supportive board, and various home-based missionaries working with me. MIA also had an arm of the ministry called Missionaries In Action. This arm of MIA took care of missionaries working in various countries, making it possible for them to do what God had called them to do. We took care of processing their support, creating their newsletters and mailing them, as well as prayer covering and other supportive services.

In August 2007 Leif's Personal Assistant resigned. My husband and I moved to Alabama with a one-year commitment to assist Leif in bringing Global Mission Awareness (GMA) to a new level as Father was spreading out GMA's tent pegs and firming up its foundation, enlarging Leif's ministry through greater favor.

"Leanne, where do you stand in the GMA family?"

After being with GMA as Leif's Personal Assistant for nine months, he asked me, "Leanne, where do you stand in this family?" I was somewhat confused by his question. I said, "I don't know what you mean." He again said, "Where do you stand within the GMA family?" I responded, "I'm your Personal Assistant, I don't know what you're talking about." Then he said, "I want to father you." Well that jerked my chain. I had heard that language between he and Paul and Ahlmira Yadao, his spiritual son and daughter in the Philippines. They would call him "Daddy Leif," or send an email to him as Daddy Leif. I would think to myself, "That is weird. Why do they call him Daddy Leif?"

At the moment of his question I began to cry. I knew that another chamber in my heart was being rummaged through. You see...I believe Papa God has created each of us with many chambers in our hearts—for our spouse, children, father and mother, brothers and sisters, other family members, very close friends, and people we are in covenant relationship with.

I realized in that moment the chamber in my heart for my biological father had never been opened. This man was now prying open the chamber door of my heart reserved for my biological father. Leif began stirring up the dust and cobwebs that had been there for fifty-two years. Though I had received much healing ministry over the years in various settings, Papa God was going much deeper. It was very painful. I told him, "I'm not ready to call you Daddy Leif." In his graciousness he said, "That's ok." At that moment, Leif became my spiritual father and began to father me. I didn't understand the dynamics at that moment, but this was something I had longed for all my life.

The next few months were some of the most painful months of my life. I would cry out to Father God, "Why are you doing this? Why do I need a spiritual father? You're my Father!" He, as well as Daddy Leif, was so very patient with me during that season.

My Spiritual Inheritance

It's been many years now, and I'm so thankful I didn't respond to Leif's request, though I wanted to, with "No thanks! I'm not interested." or "I don't see my need for a spiritual father."

Previously, a spiritual father to me was Leo Humphrey, whom I adored and respected very much. Leo fathered me regarding missions and lost souls. Leo took Ray and I on our first mission trip to Honduras in 1982. Leo died a couple of years before this conversation with Leif. I knew Papa God was now ready to take me to a new, deeper level with a spiritual father.

Prior to joining the GMA family, even with my own ministry, I knew I had hit a ceiling regarding ministry and fulfilling my Designed Destiny. I was told by my spiritual brother, Paul Yadao, shortly after becoming Leif's spiritual daughter, "Leanne, fathers hold the key to unlock the hearts of their sons and daughters, releasing them into their destiny." That made so much sense to me and resonated deep within my being. I knew this was one of the reasons I needed a spiritual father. No father had held the key to my heart, unlocking and releasing me to the fulfillment of my Designed Destiny.

At that time, I had been to twenty-one nations and experienced many situations and adventures that I am blessed to share in this book. But in order to soar higher and farther, to receive more nations and my inheritance (See Psalms 2: 7 & 8), I needed a father. I have learned more from my spiritual father, Daddy Leif, over these last several years than I had over the ten years prior.

Today Leif fathers me as an Esther receiving nations of people who are not my own. I am honored to stand before kings and pharaohs carrying the favor of the Kingdom of our God.

I am so thankful that Papa God chose to give me Leif as my spiritual father. I have such a powerful family heritage. Leif, who carries a strong anointing and love like no other person I know, is my spiritual father. Mama Jen Hetland makes anyone around her feel welcomed and loves hosting and serving. Mama Jen never meets a stranger. Papa Jack Taylor is my spiritual grandfather who carries profound Kingdom wisdom. Papa Jack's wife, Oma (grandmother in German) Friede Taylor, is my spiritual grandmother who ministers from a heart of great grace and compassion. My spiritual brother, Paul Yadao, receives holy revelation straight from the heart of Father God, as David the psalmist did. My brother Todd had the heart of Jonathan, and understood covenant relationships. I also have some absolutely amazing spiritual sons and daughters throughout the nations that are representing the Kingdom of God from a position of Sonship.

The list goes on and on and I'm so blessed to be a part of this amazing family. Having Papa Jack and Oma Friede is so valuable to me since I did not have the privilege of having a grandfather or grandmother present in my life growing up. I missed out on not only being fathered, but also grandfathered and grandmothered. Not anymore!!!

I'm thankful to Daddy Leif for all he's taught me, shown me, and what's to come. He's been so patient with me at times when I wanted to run away, when I came into this family kicking and screaming. AND, I'm especially thankful that he's taught me to See Through Heaven's Eyes.

FOUR

ORPHAN OR SON/DAUGHTER

But as many as received Him,
to them He gave the right to become children of God,
even to those who believe in His name.
~ JOHN 1:12 ~

From Sonship To Savior

Jesus referred to God as Father one hundred and forty-nine times in the Gospels. It is apparent that Jesus knew His Father, first and foremost as a father, before he knew Him as Creator, Ruler, Judge...or God. Before God was any of these, He was first Father. Before Jesus was Messiah, Savior, Miracle Worker...He was a son. Jesus was always in His Father's heart and loved by His Father.

As a result of the affirmation and love of His Father, Jesus was equipped to fulfill his Designed Destiny. So many people are wandering aimlessly, including Christians in the church, who will die never knowing, much less fulfilling, their God-given destiny. Many of these people never had a dad who unlocked the destiny in their hearts through a loving relationship and affirmation.

Nearly one in three American children are living without a

Nearly one in three American children are living without a father in their lives. father in their lives. These fathers are either totally absent from their children's lives, or present but not involved. I believe this is the most devastating crisis we have in America.

I also believe there are two heartbreaks that can be very difficult to totally heal from and get past. I know the healing power of God is all-sufficient, but please hear me out.

The first heartbreak I believe one finds very hard to get beyond is the loss of a child. I know of a few couples that have lost a child from sickness or accidents. These individuals are now living thriving lives for the Kingdom of God, and they love Him with all their hearts. But I also know that, even through counseling and years of processing their loss, there is still to this day a sting of pain in their hearts. There are those little moments and situations that remind them of that beloved child, and a flood of emotions will well up within them. It subsides, and they move forward.

The reason I believe a parent never gets one hundred percent healed from this loss is because that child was a part of their very being and carried their DNA. That child was the very essence of who they were as a parent to him or her. Something in the lineage gets cut-off, leaving a huge void never to be filled, no matter how many other children they may give birth to.

The other heartbreak I believe one never fully gets beyond is being sorely rejected by their biological father. Every person I talk with who has been rejected or abandoned by his or her father indicates the result was a huge *father wound*.

I know this heartbreak from first-hand experience. Like the one-third of the children living in America fatherless, I know what it feels like to never know one's father. Being fatherless left a gigantic void in my life that even at the age of sixty-one, still leaves me baffled. How any parent could reject their own child is totally beyond my understanding and comprehension. That child carries their parent's DNA, and when a father rejects a child, that DNA is distorted leaving that child confused and at a loss in life.

As a note, I do not want to minimize motherlessness issues. Not having a mother in ones' life can also be very difficult. I know of several people who lost their moms at a young age, leaving a major impact on their lives as in the life of Jessie:

> When I was fifteen years old my mom was diagnosed with a rare blood disease. For the next three years, I watched her fight it through dietary and lifestyle changes, chemo and radiation treatments, and eventually an adult stem cell transplant. Just months before my graduation from high school, she went home to be with the Lord.
>
> I had grown up in the church and had a relationship with the Lord since I was saved at age six. However, I was unable to deal with the emotional pain I felt. On the way to the hospital to see my mom, I would feel myself steel my emotions so that I wouldn't break down and cry when I saw her. She had enough pain and suffering to deal with, and I knew it would hurt her even more to know how much pain her illness was causing me.

I continued to stuff and numb my pain even after my mom's death. For years after she died, I rode the broken record of my unresolved grief. In my pain, I had taken on the identity of a motherless daughter and felt as though that experience was going to define me for the rest of my life. I was afraid to let go of the pain because it was all I had left of my mother, or so I thought. But as long as I held onto the pain, all I could remember was the torturous, sad memories, or the memories we never made...the things we never had a chance to do. I felt cheated that my mom missed my high school and college graduations and that she would never see me get married, or hold my children in her arms. Just as I was reaching that age where she could become not just a mom but also a friend, she was jerked out of my life.

For a long time, I refused to admit that I was angry about my mom's death. I felt that to be angry was to doubt God's goodness and to not trust Him. I so badly wanted to represent Him well and to show others how faithful He was to me. But then strange things started happening. I would spend time around older friends who had little girls of their own. I loved being with them and playing with the girls, but when one of them would get hurt and run crying to her mother, something inside me didn't want her to be able to run into her mother's arms. I wanted her to have to handle it on her own. I didn't express this, but it greatly disturbed me because I loved these little girls and I truly didn't wish them to suffer alone. I couldn't understand where these feelings were coming from until one day the Lord showed me I was angry that I lost my mom. The feelings of not wanting them to be able to run to their mommies when they were hurt were caused by my anger that I couldn't run to my mom when I was having a bad day or not feeling well.

One morning I sat out on the patio of the house I lived in and finally cried and cried and admitted that I was an angry little girl who wanted her momma back. I don't recall an amazing encounter with Jesus in that moment, but those feelings of misplaced anger did begin to subside. However, though I had dealt with my anger about my mom's death, I still felt abandoned and left behind. Some days I cried because I didn't really remember what it was like to have a mom. I felt alone and like I had the responsibility to go out and prove to everyone that I could rise out of the ashes on my own. At my core, I still believed I was a motherless daughter.

It wasn't until four years after my mom's death that I had a series of encounters with the Lord that freed me from that victim identity of being a motherless daughter. I was working at Teen Challenge at the time and the students and staff members who lived in the house had gathered together in the living room for an impromptu worship session. A coworker of mine was playing her guitar and everyone was singing a song based on Isaiah 6.

As the chorus of voices filled the room, I closed yes and saw the throne room of heaven. I quit singing and just soaked it in. Suddenly, I decided to do something crazy that I had never done. Silently, I asked the Lord to show me a glimpse of my momma. I wanted just one peek at where she was, and what she was doing. Then I saw her there in the throne room. She was standing in front of Father's throne dressed in white with her arms in the air. A huge grin was on her face and she was dancing around and around the throne. When I was a child, my mom and I used to put on messianic Jewish worship music and dance around the island in our kitchen. She was dancing just like that, but it was around the throne of God.

In that moment, I realized that my mom was not taken from me. She didn't abandon me. She didn't leave me behind. She went on ahead. She fought the good fight, kept the faith, and finished the race. And now she is dancing before her Father, my Father, waiting for me to come join her and dance together before His throne. I cannot describe the healing and freedom that revelation brought to my heart. I have not been the same since.

There are also situations where a child's father is absent due to death. This surely is devastating to a child as in the story of Savanna.

I grew up in North East Georgia about an hour from Atlanta. I lived in a Christian home with amazing parents; my father, Loy, and my mother, Johanna. Together we attended church every Sunday morning, Sunday night, and every special service that was held. God was also a huge part of our lives, even outside of church. I remember growing up, how every single time my family would be together, Jesus always came up during our conversation. His presence would come and rest in the car as we spoke about Him, even right in the middle of dinner. To this day these are some of my favorite moments when I'm with my family. From this lifestyle of daily communion with the Lord, I learned from a young age how to depend on Him no matter what the circumstances would be.

My father worked full time as a masonry foreman. While he wasn't working his masonry job, he was on call as a volunteer firefighter for both Banks County Fire Department, and Bold Springs Fire Department in Franklin County Georgia. He had a passion to serve and help people, and fighting fires was one of his avenues of doing that.

It was New Year's Eve, 1998, and I was nine years old. This night my parents had left me with my grandparents—Nanny and Papa. I remember playing with my cousins at Nanny and Papa's; putting on a big musical performance for our grandparents with spatulas, spoons, coke boxes, harmonicas, and pretend microphones. We were also talking to Papa and great uncle about how they could get initiated into our club. We were having a blast. It was just another night.

Just another night—until the phone rang. It was just past 10:00pm when Nanny answered the phone. I'm still not sure what all was said on the other end, but I do remember my Nanny's countenance changing so abruptly from happy to despondent. She slammed down the phone and flung her hands over her face. We all began to press her as to what was wrong. With hardly any strength to say what she had just heard, she lifted her head and blurted out, "Loy's trapped in a fire!" and covered her face again to catch the tears. I immediately started screaming as we all rushed to find shoes and coats to leave the house.

When we arrived at the scene I could see a large fire up the hill from the car. It was a Methodist Church set on fire by an arsonist who was a proclaimed Satan worshipper. I was taken into the fellowship hall that was about fifty feet from the church. Myself and several other people gathered together and prayed for my father that he would be safe. As the night progressed and I didn't hear any news of how he was doing or where he was at, I began to cry, "I don't want to hear bad news; only good news mama. Please don't tell me bad news. I only want to hear good news."

We left the fire and went back to my grandparent's house where, by that time, my whole extended family had gathered. I remember so vividly being cradled in my mama's lap pleading with her to not tell me bad news, only good news. Suddenly there was a weird hush that came over the entire room as my mama whispered to me, "I have something to tell you baby." As tears flooded my cheeks and anxiety gripped my heart, I pleaded with her one last time, "Please don't tell me bad news mama. I only want to hear good news." With tears streaming down her face she softly spoke, "Your daddy is gone baby."

My sobs echoed in the heart of Jesus that night, as I lay bare before him broken. My whole life had crumbled right in front of me and there was nothing I could do about it. A sweet, nine-year-old girl was now fatherless because of tragedy. I didn't know what to do.

Less than a year after my dad was promoted to heaven, I started attending church other nights of the week on my own accord. I would have a family member go with me or drop me off. I was ten years old and attending youth group at one church on Monday nights, and another on Wednesday nights. I also kept going to church Sunday morning, Sunday night, and any other time I could get a ride somewhere. I didn't care what church I went to, what the service was for, or who attended. I just wanted to be in the presence of Jesus because it was only there that I didn't feel alone.

During some of these meetings I began to have great encounters with the Lord. The more I reached for His heart, the more He healed mine. It was then that I realized He was my Father. Not just the Father, by my Father. This revelation opened a whole new side of God's heart to me. I gained so much healing just in realizing His heart for me as His daughter. I didn't have to be fatherless anymore. My identity wasn't the girl who lost her father. My identity was a daughter of the King.

During this season of my life, in the beginning stages of my healing, Jesus began to deal with my heart about forgiving the man who set the fire that ultimately killed my dad. The idea of forgiving this man was hard for me. It seemed so contrary to justice, so opposite of fair. Why should I have to forgive someone who truly wronged me? I was rightfully angry. He didn't deserve anything but to die, I thought. But my spirit cried out within me knowing I couldn't enter God's kingdom with unforgiveness in my heart. I longed to be right with God more than I longed to be justified in my anger and bitterness. I cried out to my Daddy asking Him to help me forgive this man.

As I wrestled with the truth that unforgiveness would keep me from His kingdom, the Lord spoke one thing to me that broke the barrier in my heart, which kept me from forgiving. He said, "Savanna, what happens if that man repents to me and you see him in heaven one day? What will you do with all that bitterness you have toward him?" I was immediately taken to my knees as I repented to God and forgave this man. I have been living free from the bondage of unforgiveness ever since. It is my prayer that one day I will be able to visit him in prison, let him know I forgive him, and tell him how much Jesus loves him!

As days, months, and years went by, I had to deal with the fear that—just as my earthly father was suddenly gone, possibly the same thing would happen with my heavenly Father; He would just suddenly not be there. Jesus came and crushed that lie and showed me that even though I had lost my earthly father, I wasn't going to lose my heavenly Father. He is God and His faithfulness and security to me isn't based on my experience, but on His nature.

While I have lacked an earthly father for security, identity, protection and leadership, I have not been deprived all together. Though I didn't have an earthly father to provide those things, I have a heavenly Father who did. There were many times throughout the years where I faced overwhelming emotions of my dad being gone and feeling like my world had been destroyed. During those times, God would come to me and reestablish in the depths of my soul that I was His precious daughter. Many days, or even seasons, I struggled with my identity and knowing who I was. Time and time again, without delay, He would speak truth to my heart and overthrow every lie from the enemy. I can look back now and see all the times He kept me from harm, just as any father would have done. Through every struggle I've had, His leadership has been perfect in my life.

As much pain that my father's passing brought me, it also brought me to a place of dependence on God as

Father, to which I never would have otherwise come to. It was the revelation of God as my Father that has kept me these years. Without God's role as Father in my life, I never would have made it through my devastating loss.

Statistics show that in our society fatherlessness is at a high rate and very devastating. A child left fatherless due to rejection, or death, can be an all-out deathblow to that child if that child does not have the revelation of God being a Father to him or her.

Look with me at the facts and consequences of fatherlessness in our country alone. But first let's define what an orphan is:

Orphan –
    a. *A child whose parents are dead.*
    b. *Deprived of parents.*
    c. *One that lacks support, supervision, or care.*

If we take into fact the last two definitions of an orphan, this is the gross reality we're facing today per the statistics below:

THE FACTS OF "FATHERLESSNESS"

⌘ The percentage of kids born out-of-wedlock has grown 223% since 1970. (US Department of Health and Human Services, 2005)

⌘ 7 out of 10 African-American kids are born out-of-wedlock. (US Department of Health and Human Services, 2005)

⌘ 3 out of 10 Caucasian kids are born out-of-wedlock, an increase of 440% since 1970. (US Department of Health and Human Services, 2005)

THE CONSEQUENCES

⌘ 90% of homeless and runaway children are from fatherless homes – 32 times the average. (US Department of Health and Human Services, Bureau of the Census)

⌘ 80% of rapists motivated with displaced anger come from fatherless homes – 14 times the average. (Justice and Behavior, Vol. 14, p. 403-26, 1987)

⌘ 60% of repeat rapists grew up without fathers. (Raymond A Knight and Robert A. Prentky, "The Developmental Antecedents of Adult Adaptations of Rapist Sub-Types, "Justice and Behavior, Vol. 14, 1987, p. 403-426)

⌘ 71% of pregnant teenagers lack a father. (US Department of Health and Human Services press release, Friday, March 26, 1999)

⌘ 63% of youth suicides are from a fatherless home. (US Department of Health and Human Services, Bureau of the Census)

⌘ 85% of children who exhibit behavioral disorders

come from fatherless homes. (Center for Disease Control)

⌘ 90% of adolescent repeat arsonists live with only their mother. (Wray Herbert, "Dousing the Kindlers", Psychology Today, January 1985, p 28)

⌘ 71% of high school dropouts come from fatherless homes. (National Principals Association Report on the State of High Schools)

⌘ 75% of adolescent patients in chemical abuse centers come from fatherless homes – 10 times the average. (Rainbow for all God's Children)

⌘ 70% of youth in state operated institutions come from fatherless homes – 9 times the average. (US Department of Justice, September 1988)

⌘ 85% of youth in prisons come from fatherless homes – 20 times the average. (Fulton County Georgia, Texas Department of Corrections)

⌘ 75% of prisoners grew up without a father. (Daniel Amneus, The Garbage Generation, Alhambra, CA: Primrose Press, 1990)

⌘ Fatherless boys and girls are twice as likely to drop out of high school, twice as likely to end up in jail, four times more likely to need help with emotional or behavioral problems. (US Department of Health and

Human Services news release, March 26, 1999)
⌘ 43% of US children live without their father. (US Department of Census)

The devil comes to steal, kill, and destroy. He will do whatever it takes to keep us from fulfilling our God-given Designed Destiny. As I mentioned at the start of this book, I can look back through the chapters of my life and see clearly the times the devil tried to take me out and/or shut me down. He knew Whose I was and what I was created to do in this world.

I can still remember when I began to receive the truth that the man living in our house, that I called dad, was clearly not my biological father. It also became clear that my two older brothers were not his biological sons, either. His name was Claude Mc Collough. My two older brothers were Eddie and Billy Crawley. My two younger brothers were Frank and Chet Mc Collough.

I was around twelve years old, a period in a child's life when the covering and affirmation of their father is of extreme, vital importance. I was preparing to enter junior high school when this revelation began to unfold in my young life. These dynamics in our house were rarely ever spoken of.

FIVE

THE AGE OF TWELVE

And when he was twelve years old,
they went up to Jerusalem after the custom of the feast.
~ LUKE 2:42 ~

A Critical Transition

I want you to be aware of my age when the impact of Claude not being my biological father hit me, the age of *twelve*. I believe the age of *twelve* has significant importance for each of us. Around this age is when a child usually goes through a critical transition in their life. A few years ago, I did a study on the age of *twelve*. I found that *twelve* years of age in a child's life, for many cultures, is an important and

> *I believe the age of twelve has significant importance for each of us.*

vulnerable period. This is a period of life when a boy or a girl steps into the beginning stages preparing them for adulthood, i.e. a girl begins her menstrual cycle preparing her for womanhood. Boys begin their own body changes preparing them for manhood.

✪ Jesus was *twelve* years old when He was reading the scriptures in the temple. He was in transition. His transition was regarding Kingdom matters. After this incident, we do not hear anything of his earthly father, Joseph, again. God, Jesus'

Father, becomes the greater influencer in His life. He told his parents that He had to be about His "Father's" business. His Designed Destiny was beginning to unfold at this early age. Like Jesus, I believe around the age of *twelve* each person goes through a time of transition that begins to mold and shape him or her for their Kingdom purpose.

It also says Jesus was separated from his parents, (See Luke 2:41S52). Ancient Jews did not practice the Bar Mitzvah. They practiced the Mishnah, the reading of the scriptures. If the Mishna is relevant to the first-century Jewish practice, which is likely in this case, then religious instruction would have become more intense for Jesus upon his reaching *twelve* (m. Niddah 5:6; m. Megilla 4:6; m. `Abot 5:12).

There are specific details about bar/bat mitzvah's and the historical significance of the ceremony done for boys at age thirteen, girls at *twelve*. However, it requires one year of preparation before the ceremony. So, boys are *twelve* years old when they start the curriculum. It's believed from Luke's account of Jesus in the temple (See Luke 2:41-45), that this was a type of bar mitzvah. This term didn't exist until the middle ages, but in ancient Jewish culture, *twelve*-year-old boys went to the feasts with their parents and took on other religious duties just as the bar mitzvah does, (Bar mitzvah = son of the commandments, bat = daughter (Hebrew) bar is Aramaic).

The present custom of bar mitzvah for a thirteen-year-old Jewish boy was not in place at that time, (Fitzmyer 1981:440).

(http://www.biblegateway.com/resources/commentaries/IV
PSNT/Luke/Twelve-Year-Old-Jesus-Goes),
(http://jbuff.com/c032901.htm).

✪ The number *twelve* in the Bible represents government.
Jesus was representing the government of heaven when He
was in the temple reading from the scriptures. We, too, are to
represent the government of heaven here on earth. Matthew
6:10 says, "Thy kingdom come. Thy will be done in earth, as it
is in heaven."

Leif Hetland, my spiritual father, is known to surely represent
heaven, or the government of heaven, here on earth. Anyone
who knows Leif is aware of his assignment of bringing
transformation to the nations of the earth, one being the
most spiritually dark nation on this planet.

At the age of *twelve*, Leif experienced a shameful violation,
and as a result caused him to run from God. For several years,
Leif attempted to numb the pain of this abuse through drugs
and alcohol, living on the streets and in parks. One day the
prodigal son went home to his Father and became a son...a
son that is a lover of God and a lover of people.

Leif is now a "bulldozer," plowing through some of the
darkest, most closed-off nations on the earth with the Good
News of Jesus.

The enemy attempted to steal, rob, and destroy the Designed
Destiny on Leif Hetland's life, as I'm convinced he does with
all of us. But today Leif is fulfilling his Designed Destiny,

representing heaven on earth through extravagant love, signs, wonders, and miracles. (You can read more about Leif Hetland in his books: Seeing Through Heaven's Eyes, Healing the Orphan Spirit, and Baptism of Love.)

✪ Samuel was *twelve* years old when the Lord called to him three times in the night (See I Samuel 3).

✪ Manasseh was *twelve* years old when he became king and reigned fifty-five years in Jerusalem (See 2 Chronicles 33).

✪ Many theologians believe Mary was probably around thirteen when the angel Gabriel visited her. (http://www.vineyardusa.org/site/taskS forces/youth/article/god/only/uses/adults/not).

✪ In the United States, the average age a girl starts her menstrual cycle is *twelve*, preparing her for womanhood. (http://womenshealth.about.com/od/menstruation/a/menst ruationfaq_4.htm).

✪ *Twelve* years of age is the most common age of puberty. Around this age, a boy or girl begins to ask the question, "What's happening to my body?"

OTHER NUMBER "TWELVE" FACTS IN SCRIPTURE:

✪ As mentioned *TWELVE* is the *perfection of government*. *Twelve* is the number of the Church, both the Old Covenant Church of Israel founded by *twelve* physical fathers (the *twelve* sons of Jacob/Israel) and the New Covenant Church founded by *twelve* spiritual fathers (the *twelve* Apostles). This number also has a relationship with multiples of *twelve*.

✪ *Twelve* signs of the zodiac (these ancient symbols are found in Jewish synagogues of the 1st century AD).

✪ The product of the number three (perfection of divinity) X four (the number of the earth).

✪ *Twelve* months in a year.

✪ *Twelve* tribes of Israel (See Genesis 49:28).

✪ *Twelve* pillars were erected at Mt. Sinai (See Exodus 24:4).

✪ *Twelve* pillars were erected in the Promised Land (See Joshua 4:1-9).

✪ *Twelve* statues of oxen held up the water basin in Solomon's Temple (See 1 Kings 7:25).

✪ *Twelve* men were selected by God to conduct the census of the tribes (See Numbers 1:2-16).

✪ *Twelve* princes of Israel brought gifts to the Sanctuary on *twelve* days (See Numbers 7:10-83).

✪ *Twelve* spies sent to spy out Canaan (See Numbers 13:1-15).

✪ Jesus is *twelve* years old when He questions the scholars in the Temple (See Luke 2:41).

✪ *Twelve* legions of angels (See Matthew 26:53).

✪ *Twelve* Apostles (See Matthew 10:2-4; Mark 3:13-19; Luke 6:13).

✪ *Twelve* gates of the New Jerusalem (See Revelation 21:12).

✪ *Twelve* foundations of the New Jerusalem (See Revelation 21:16, 17).

✪ The Trees of Life in the new creation will bear *twelve* kinds of fruit (See Revelation 22:2).

As you can see, *twelve* is a significant number. The Lord called Samuel at the age of *twelve*. I believe the Devil is also calling out to *twelve* year olds to lead them astray from fulfilling their Designed Destiny, as was the case with Bill Reiser, a former New York basketball legend who played for Eastern Kentucky University.

I was once at the local post office in their bulk-mailing room preparing to mail GMA's annual Christmas newsletter when I heard Bill's story. The clerk had a radio tuned in to a local radio station. When Bill talked about a violation in his life at the age of *twelve*, my ears perked up. The clerk, noticing I was possibly distracted by what was being broadcast over the radio said, "Is that bothering you? I can turn it off." My response, "Oh no, please don't turn it off. Who is this guy and what station is this you're listening to?" I took out a pen and paper and began taking notes as I listened to Bill. The two words he used that primarily caught my attention were identity and destiny.

Bill mentioned that he went through a series of events when he was *twelve* years old that shaped the pattern of behavior of who he was going to be for the first thirty-six years of his life.

Like me, Bill's father left him, his mother, and two sisters when he was six months old. Bill never again saw or heard from his father. Bill used basketball, alcohol, drugs, and women to numb the pain in his life. Here's Bill's story as told in his amazing book, <u>Vertical Leap, HOW JESUS CHANGED NEW YORK CITY BASKETBALL LEGEND BILL RIESER, by Moody Publishers, 2009.</u>

Innocence Lost

The summer of 1972 was a black summer for me. The dark side of East Harlem where I grew up extinguished any ray of innocence still in me. I had grown up without a dad and had struggled to survive on the streets. When my mom was working late on some job trying to help us survive, as a little boy of twelve years old I'd take to the streets.

The place was infested with bad characters, like the Mob guys and the Mob wannabes. Then there were the general misfits—angry teenagers already dead on the inside who found pleasure in bullying and hurting people, especially the young and weak. They carried knives and guns and were always on a short fuse.

I'd seen what they could do; you didn't mess with

them. *If you saw those angry punks on your side of the street, you crossed over. But you couldn't avoid them if they were blocking your doorway or the gate to the park. Then you caught their attitude and lip and a few punches. This was the life I knew, so I did not think much about it. Later I realized how fear released a constant rush of adrenaline in me.*

That July afternoon was like most summer days in East Harlem. The sun scorched the concrete and asphalt until the heat burned your feet through your sneakers. My friends and I would walk to Ronnie's candy shop on 1st Avenue between 114th and 115th, pull a cold soda from the coolers, pay our 25 cents, then move along the street sipping the bottle. If you drank it too fast, the chilled liquid made your head hurt.

That afternoon I'd ended up with a friend in his apartment on 115th street. As I ran down the last flight of stairs and opened the door to the brownstone's entrance area, a young man stepped from the shadows and pressed a blade into my neck. My heart raced. I knew this guy—like many others in the hood, who by their late teens had surrendered to the demons of the street "You gonna do what I want you to, Billy," he whispered, jabbing me. The steel glistened in the half dark. I was at his mercy, for at that time of day, it might be an hour or more before anyone came or left the building. In the distance, I heard car horns honking and children splashing at an open fire hydrant. Here it was quiet, except for the rasp of his breath.

"Get down on your knees." I saw contempt in his eyes. Why did he hate me so much? I hardly knew him. Digging the knife into my neck, he sexually abused me.

I hated it but did what he asked me to do. He told me if I told anyone he'd kill me and he'd kill my family. No one came into the entryway to rescue me. I trembled, tears staining my cheeks. Would he return? Scrambling to my feet, I cracked the apartment door. He was gone. Shaking with shame, fear and rage, I walked warily home along the hot streets. Shame overwhelmed me and I was hit with an identity crisis. I did not know who I was. A pain started growing inside of me like an emotional cancer.

I told no one what had happened. What good would it do? He might come back to cut me or maybe even hurt my mother. I fantasized for years what it would be like to catch him and slit his throat. Good that in the meantime I met God and surrendered my lust for revenge.

That same summer I became a drug runner for another thug in our neighborhood, Johnny. He was the most feared guy in our neighborhood. No one knows how many people Johnny had killed.

Another tragic moment in my terrible 1972 hadn't helped. I was forced to have sex with a prostitute. Such an experience does not encourage a healthy appreciation of women. I assumed that manhood equaled sex from that day forward.

I have done much counseling throughout my years of ministry, especially during the ten years we were with Teen Challenge. As I would ask many men and women, "Tell me, was there anything that took place in your life between the ages of eleven to thirteen, but more specifically around the age of *twelve*?" It was stunning when the person reflected to that period in their life and what they remembered. This would happen repeatedly—the death of a parent, or their parents divorced, or mom left, or dad left, they were physically or sexually abused, or extremely humiliated.

I remember one story of a friend of mine. Because of the stronghold of pornography in his life, I said to him, "I want you to think back to when you were between the ages of eleven to thirteen years old. Was there a particular incident that took place in your life that might be relative to your pornography abuse today?" It's almost as if you could hear the bell go off in his head. He began to pour out the scene to me.

When he was *twelve* years old, he was walking across a field in the area he lived. He came across a magazine. When he picked it up, it was a pornographic magazine. Intrigued and caught, he went to a tree house and gazed through the magazine for hours.

There is a window of vulnerability at the age of *twelve* (or somewhere between eleven and thirteen) where I believe the enemy targets a child to distort their perception of God and steal, kill, and destroy their purpose and destiny. The is the age where a child is at their most vulnerable stage of life.

There is a window of vulnerability at the age of twelve.

At the age of *twelve* is:

⌘ When a child's body begins to develop and change. Hormones begin to burst forth.

⌘ When dad's influence begins to take on a stronger role than their mom's. I had a friend share with me recently that her middle son was giving some thought as to a decision he needed to make about a matter in his life. She gave him her opinion, then he answered, "Well that's good mom, but I want to see what dad thinks." Now this boy has a very close relationship with his mom, but at *twelve* years of age, his dad's opinion carried a heavier weight for him than mom's.

I believe mom has a greater influence of nurturing a child until the age of *twelve*; dad has a greater influence of guiding them beyond the age of *twelve*. Mom rears and then dad steers. Of course, this is not absolute, but in my years of ministry, I've perceived this to be the case more times than not.

⌘ When a father becomes more responsible for a daughter's virginity.

⌘ When a child is transitioning from grade school to middle school, becoming more vulnerable.

⌘ In grade school girls have "cooties", and kids don't care much of how they dress. In middle school girls become awesome and kids begin to "keep up with the

Jones".

⌘ At the age of *twelve* is when most sexual assaults and rape occur. (http://www.rainn.org/get-information/statistics/frequency/of/sexual/assault)

SIX

FROM VICTIM TO VICTOR

There is no fear in love;
but perfect love casteth out fear: because fear hath torment.
He that feareth is not made perfect in love.
~I JOHN 4:18 ~

Perfect Love Casts Out Fear

Consider with me the story of Lori, a beautiful daughter of Father God, who was created to love. Through abuse, fear paralyzed her life:

> *My thirteenth birthday is one that will always linger in the recesses of my mind. I do not recall celebrating this event with some elaborate birthday party, although I'm sure it was celebrated. I just can't recall the celebration for the overpowering thought of how the day began. Instead of feeling the anticipation and excitement of becoming a teenager, I was feeling the anxiety of my next visit to the Mental Health Center for another counseling session. I will never forget sitting in that cold office with a lady who kept asking me all these questions about my daddy, who by the way, was a prince of a dad. The events in my life that led me to this lady's office was not at the hands of my father, but rather the hands of a much older cousin.*

The summer I turned twelve years old I was sexually molested and the enemy launched an all-out attack to ultimately end my life. For the next seven years, he had full reign and came at me with full force.

I was raised in a loving home with both parents. They were very much involved in my sister's life and mine. We had a home filled with laughter and fun. I was blessed with my dad's sense of humor. I had a captive audience with my mom and dad. My parents seemed to genuinely enjoy my presence. I never felt I was in the way and I do not recall ever being pushed aside for any reason. I loved my life. Looking back now, the only thing we were missing as a family was church.

I wasn't raised in the Word of God, so when the enemy showed up in my life, we simply didn't recognize him. He slowly began to suck the life out of me the year I turned twelve.

During that year, I did a 180° turn on the inside of me, and my personality began to reflect it. I was gripped with a spirit of fear. I went from being a carefree little girl, to an over 'protector of my little sister and myself. I began having extremely violent nightmares and I was horribly paranoid anytime I was away from my dad. The enemy convinced me that every man that looked at me twice was going to follow us home to kill me, or worse, my entire family. I would lie in bed at night and literally be paralyzed with fear of going to sleep. I would close my eyes and see images of angry faced men. I still remember the faces today. I was so afraid of the dark I would turn my bedroom light off at the door and jump from the door to my bed so I didn't have to walk close to my bed in case someone was hiding under it. I was simply too fearful to check for peace of mind. I wouldn't allow my arm to hang over the side of the bed either because I feared someone grabbing it.

I had thoughts of suicide regularly and feelings of helplessness and certainly hopelessness. I thought I would have to live like that for the rest of my life. The feeling of shame and disgust began to overtake me. I felt guilty for what happened to me. The enemy has a way of placing false blame and unmerited shame on the innocent. So, out of feelings of fault, I kept this secret and pushed it under what I call my invisible rug. When my mom and I went anywhere without my dad, fear would overtake me. I was constantly watching everyone around us. My family joked about how I would be a great eye witness to a crime because I could look at a person one time and remember everything they were wearing down to the type of shoes they had on, hair color, facial features and even eye color if they were close enough to me. What my family didn't realize is I was observing people like they had committed a crime, because I was convinced they were going to commit one against us. If a man got behind us in line at the grocery store, I would start saying, "Dad will be home when we get there, won't he? "or "If we don't get home soon dad will be looking for us." I'm sure some of those innocent bystanders thought I had an abusive, controlling father, but out of fear I felt I was letting them know my dad would get them if they tried to hurt me.

My mom and dad saw the changes in me and I know they were trying their best to help, but I was a locked vault when they asked me questions about my behavior. They really tried to get me to tell them what was going on. Out of fear I would become very defensive and shut the conversation down, because I thought I had done something wrong.

My behavior began to affect every area of my life, and fear began to control my entire family. One afternoon my mom, my sister and I went to lunch with a friend of the family and her children. I remember feeling the anxiety building up in me when we pulled into the parking lot of the restaurant. My stomach was in knots. As we were walking in the restaurant a man approached the door at the same time and tripped on the step at the door. Immediately, in my judgment, I concluded he was drunk and up to no good. I was convinced if he were to do something to anyone, it would be to us. So, my radar went to work watching his every move.

I will never forget the feeling of my heart pounding in my chest as fear slowly tortured me into a full` blown panic attack. We had just sat down with our food. Everyone started eating and I kept watching this man. Realistically, he was looking around the crowded restaurant for a vacant table. To an overprotective, fear 'infested adolescent, I was convinced he was *planning an attack on my family.*

I kicked into full panic mode and started telling my mother we needed to get out of the restaurant right away. Like any other mother would do, she began to try and calm me down by reassuring me we were ok. In my mind, she didn't understand what this man was going to do, so I took matters into my own hands. I started frantically throwing everyone's food in the garbage can. With no food left on the table to eat, lunch was over. I know that must have embarrassed my mother immensely, to say the least, but she graciously accepted my strong suggestion to leave the restaurant. After all, it was for our safety, right?

That was the day my mom realized her little girl needed help beyond her capabilities. She and my dad contacted the Mental Health Center for an appointment to get me counseling. They really tried, but I was unwilling to pull the invisible rug back and talk about what was hidden under it. So, my thirteenth birthday marked my last session with a counselor.

During the next few years my sense of humor became a mask I hid behind, away from home. I made a joke of everything that hurt or scared me so my friends wouldn't think anything was wrong with me. At home, I'm sure I was beginning to get very hateful and unpleasant to be around.

Over the course of seven years, fear had its way in my life and some of my worst fears came to pass. At sixteen-years old I was raped. By the age of eighteen I was violated again which resulted in an abortion that was pushed under my invisible rug. The thoughts of suicide were overwhelming and self-hatred had worked its way into the picture. The day I was driven to the abortion clinic, a part of me died. I was told there was no other option for me. The one thing I had adamantly declared I would never do, I did. I felt I could not live with that decision, and the enemy reinforced the thought daily.

A few weeks later I was simply invited to church with a friend. I knew the moment the invite was given, that was the answer to my pain. I went to church the following Sunday and Jesus met me at the altar that day. I fell in love with the ultimate protector and He began a work in my heart that caused the enemy's plans to fail. Papa God spoke to my heart one morning and told me, "The enemy has come against you with a fear of man, because of your heart's ability to love others."

At twelve-years old I didn't know the plans Papa God had for my life. I didn't realize I was destined to be a minister of the gospel. I had no clue I would be married to a minister and co-pastoring a church by the age of twenty-nine. When I received Jesus as my Savior and received the baptism of the Holy Spirit at the age of nineteen, I began to tell Papa God I would do anything He wanted me to do. I was willing to go anywhere He asked me to go. I prayed a prayer of surrender and declared I was not my own. I belonged to Him and I asked Him to let my life leave a mark in this earth for His glory. I asked Him to pour His love into my heart and allow me to love others the way He does. My life began to change rapidly.

I found myself weeping and praying for people I saw walking on the side of the road. Instead of running from people I found myself being drawn to them. The love of God overtook my life. Eventually, I realized He had given me permission to do some pretty awesome things for His Kingdom and I refuse to leave this earth until every promise He has given me is played out in my life. If we have a promise from Papa God, He will bring it to pass. I encourage others to observe their deepest hurts, and to understand that their deepest pain has the potential of becoming their greatest passion. Fear brought me my deepest pain, but loving others has now become my greatest passion.

A Lost Identity

In 1987 I was sitting in a workshop at a Regional Women's Aglow Conference in Galveston, TX. I really do not remember who was speaking or what she was speaking on, but whatever the woman was speaking about, God took me back to a setting when I was approximately twelve years old. My mom and I were sitting on the couch in our living room. I really do not remember what we were talking about, but I remembered her saying, "Leanne, I love you but there is something about my boys."

I never realized the impact that statement had on my life. I was already feeling immensely rejected by my biological father. Now

I wasn't good enough for my mom, either.

There were numerous events and situations that took place in my life between the ages of eleven and twelve that left me wondering

The enemy used computer language, bolded and CAPITALIZED.

what my purpose was in life; where did I fit in; why did God create me. I believe I made some choices at that time to try and gain my mom's love that she had for my brothers. I believe at that moment is when a way of orphan thinking began to control my life. I longed for my father to want me, and my mother to love me like she did my brothers.

To this day, I know my mom loved me, and because of the knowing, I never did bring that moment on the couch in our living room up to her. I'm sure the conversation was not a conversation of rejection and disappointment toward me. But the enemy used computer language, **bolded** and CAPITALIZED, and yelled out that statement from my mom loud and clear in my heart, spirit, and mind, *"Rejection, rejection...unloved, unloved."*

I couldn't understand why my biological father did not want me—why he didn't want anything to do with me. There were many nights I would lie in my bed, in the dark and alone, crying and asking God, *"Why doesn't my dad call me? Why doesn't he want me? Why doesn't he want to see me? Why no phone call, no letter, no birthday or Christmas present? Why?"* The question always haunted me, *"What does he look like? Is he tall? Is he short? Bald?"*

I so longed for a dad who would ask me when he got home from work, "How was school today?" or have a conversation about life, tuck me in bed at night, or just hold me. I longed for a dad who would cheer me on at school events, or just say, *"You can do this. I believe in you!"*

In my heart and mind I was very confused growing up. My life was like a scrabble board trying to find the missing pieces and make some sense of my life. I would go to school and sometimes write Leanne Crawley (my legal name). Other times I would write Leanne McCollough. I wasn't sure who I really was and who I really belonged to. I remember getting a beautiful necklace for Christmas one year from my mom and stepfather that had my initials. The initials were LLM for Lois Leanne McCollough. I still have that necklace, but the point is I never was a McCollough.

It was delicious and melted in my mouth.

I had a good stepfather. Claude worked very hard to make sure my four brothers and I were well fed, clothed, and had a roof over our heads. Even though there were many rocky times in our house, I had good childhood memories that stick with me today.

My mom worked for the airlines most of my life, so this meant that we had the privileges of traveling throughout the United States and around the world. Each year we took a vacation. A couple of times we drove from New Orleans to Big Ben National Park in our two Volkswagen bugs. When I was in high school we flew to Hawaii. I'm thankful I had the opportunity to travel like I did. I'm convinced it was a designed preparation from my Father God training me for part of what I do today; hosting International Ministry Teams throughout the world.

There are other childhood memories that I cherish, like helping my mom make fresh coconut cake at Christmas. Mind you, we didn't have the bags of coconut available to us at the local grocery like we do today. We had to do everything from scratch. So, I would crack open the coconut, drain the milk from it that she'd use in the cake. Then I'd grind the meat of the coconut into flakes to sprinkle over the cake. I can taste that cake in my mouth even as I write about it. It was delicious and melted in my mouth.

Our family loved to barbecue. We had a huge stone barbecue pit in our backyard. We barbecued quite often and would have all the fixins (as one would say in the south) to go along with it. And we couldn't leave out the homemade vanilla ice cream. We didn't have Blue Bell to give us that absolute homemade taste. No, we had to labor hard to get it. No electric ice cream makers, either. We had the do-it-yourself crank style. We'd put the milk, cream, sugar, and vanilla in the inside tub. Then around the tub we'd pack ice and rock salt. Then what seemed for hours, we'd crank and crank the handle until we could feel the firmness develop with the solution eventually becoming rich and creamy.

Another childhood memory I have is going crawfishing and snake hunting with my stepfather and my brothers. Yep, you heard me right. We would wake up in the very early hours of the morning, load up in our car with nets, melt (the bait one uses to catch crawfish, or also known as mudbugs), and sacks, and go to the swamps outside of New Orleans to crawfish. Many times we'd find some snakes along the way and bring those, as well as the crawfish, home. I remember times we would boil up one hundred pounds of crawfish with corn on the cob and little new potatoes. We'd spread newspaper over our picnic table; throw those babies all over the table and get to eating. They were delicious!

Our home was always full of snakes, as well as other critters from time to time, like our raccoon, Sam. Sam lived in our house. He loved oranges and apples. He'd take an apple in his little hands and within no time devour it. Usually he would have the run of the house. He'd crawl on the back of the couch and while you were sitting down he'd begin to rummage through your hair as if he was looking for something. Eventually Sam got too big and began to show his wild side, so we had to let Sam go. I really liked that raccoon.

At one time, we had an alligator. I don't remember if we ever named the alligator, but I do remember walking him on a leash. The alligator was only about three feet long. Now mind you, we lived in a neighborhood, not out on a farm with several acres. The neighborhood we lived in, one could almost reach their arm out the window and touch the house next door. Well, not really, but I think you get the idea. So, the entire neighborhood knew the uniqueness of our family when it came to animals and reptiles. And yes, I'm sure we were considered the weird ones on the block. But all the kids liked to come to the McCollough house.

Getting back to the snakes, at any given time, our house could have up to three aquariums with snakes in them. My stepfather was very committed to not having any poisonous snakes in the house. That didn't mean they weren't around, just not in the house. I know about now you're thinking; these people were a bunch of snake handlers. Well you might say we were, but it had nothing to do with religious practices...just snakes.

As I mentioned, we did a family vacation almost yearly. During each vacation, it was a must that we visit the nearby Snake Farm, and back then there was one in just about every city we went to. Honestly, it got to the point—if you've seen one snake, you've seen them all. We would beg Claude to move on to the next attraction, which eventually he'd relent and we did.

Claude was one of those who had motherlessness issues. His mother abandoned him on Christmas day when he was a young boy. I'm not sure of his exact age, but I wouldn't be the least bit surprised if it wasn't around twelve years old. His father sent him out to the car to fetch something. When he opened the trunk of the car, his mother's suitcases were in there and she was leaving his father for another man. To this day I can still remember Christmas days when Claude would go out to the car by himself and read the newspaper for hours.

I knew Claude loved me the only way he knew how. But due to hurts and wounds from his childhood, which he carried into his marriage with my mom, he had a lot of love deficits himself. I remember one day when I was about eleven years old. The kids in the neighborhood were playing cabbage ball. If you do not know what a cabbage ball is—it's like a softball, but bigger and softer. It's about five inches in diameter and you don't use a glove to play.

Anyhow, I ran down the street to the gang and asked if I could play. One of the older boys, Johnny Martinez, said, "No". I responded, "Please. I can be permanent catcher." Johnny said, "No, but you can be permanent ass hole." I was not only embarrassed, but also devastated. I ran home crying my eyes out.

I ran home crying my eyes out.

When my stepfather heard what happened he stormed out the house ready to tear the head off Johnny Martinez, and trust me, he could have. Claude was 6'4" and didn't lack any strength. My mom had to grab him begging him not to do something he'd regret. He made his way to Johnny Martinez, giving him a piece of his mind. Johnny Martinez never bothered me again.

I remember another time when I was a senior in high school. I was suspended for three days from school. I'll spare you the details, but honestly, I had done nothing to deserve suspension. I was called to the principal's office and given my suspension slip. When I brought it home and Claude read it, he was furious because they had him down as Mr. Crawley. The next day he accompanied me to the school office. I must say Claude put the school principal in her place stating, *"If you paid more attention to your school records than trying to find out ways to suspend students that haven't warranted being suspended, you'd be running a better school."* I had my head up high as he and I walked out of that office and my suspension was removed. Those were two times that stand out in my upbringing that I felt I had a dad who had my back.

Snakes were a part of my childhood growing up

Me, my mom, and my brother Billy

At 12 years old when I realized Claude was not my father

Ray with his beautiful hair in 1974

Our wedding Day, October 18, 1974

The first and only time I ever met my dad

L-R: me, Eddie, Faye, my dad, and my sister-in-law, Joanie, 1981

My first trip to Honduras, 1982

My four brothers
L-R: Eddie, Chet, Billy, myself and Frank, 1988.

Heading to YWAM for our missionary training, 1984

Teen Challenge - Colfax, IA. 1992

Teen Challenge - Chattanooga, TN. 1998

Preaching in Cuba, 2008

Four generations: Beth, my mom, me and Zoe, 2008

Preaching in Pakistan, 2012

Blessing the beautiful women of Pakistan, 2012

Ray and Me today

SEVEN

SONS GET IT!

For the earnest expectation of the creature waiteth for the manifestation of the sons of God.
~ ROMANS 8:19 ~

Our Identities As Sons And Daughters

After Jesus was anointed by the Spirit, He was affirmed by His Father (See Matthew 3:16-17). After He was affirmed by His Father, He was tested by the devil (See Matthew 4:1-11). And after He passed His test, He was released to His assignment (See Matthew 4:12-25).

After He passed the test, He was released to His assignment.

Knowing who He was and how much He was loved by His Father made all the difference in how Jesus went about His assignment. To the degree that a child of God understands and lives from their identity as a son or daughter, will make all the difference in how they go about their assignment. From that place of connection with the love in His Father's heart—from that place where His identity and worth were not only stored, but were also treasured, empowered Jesus to fulfill His assignment.

Believing in Father's love is one thing; being baptized in it is another. That is why we use the phrase *Baptism of Love*. It's not an indoctrination, it's an immersion. Father God immerses us in His love by placing us on His lap, so to speak, where He lovingly embraces us, pressing us against His chest so closely we can hear the beats of His heart—for others, the future, the nations, and ourselves. With every swooshing beat of it, we become saturated with His indescribable love that leaves us transformed from our inner core out. He presses us close so that our heart connects with His. He keeps us close until the beat of His heart resets the beat of ours.

Once we have experienced this *Baptism of Love*, we begin to love Him with all our heart, all our soul, and all our strength. Everything changes. Everything within us—every thought, every feeling, every word, and every action—beats in rhythm with His. We begin to love others in an entirely new way, not just our friends and family, but our enemies and strangers.

The Safest Dwelling Place

Just before Moses' death, it says that he blessed the sons of Israel (See Deuteronomy 33:1). Each tribe received their blessings from Moses—to one tribe the blessing of their land, to another protection from their enemies, yet another to live and not die and his tribe would be many. But smack dab in the middle of the blessings comes this profound one, *"And of Benjamin he said, the beloved of the LORD shall dwell in safety by him; and the LORD shall cover him all day long, and he shall dwell between his shoulders."* (Deuteronomy

Can you imagine being blessed to dwell between Papa God's shoulders?

104

33:12). Wow, what a verse. Can you imagine being blessed to dwell between Papa God's shoulders? This tribe received the blessing to lean straight into the heart of God, hearing and feeling His heartbeat, His very breath on their foreheads, in security, rest, and comfort. Oh, what a place to dwell! This IS the SECRET place of the Most High, not a mountain, or a cleft in the rock.

Just as a small child climbs up into their parent's lap and receives a firm, loving embrace in a time of fear or pain and finds safety and comfort, we too can receive overwhelming love, peace and security in our Father's arms. We can nestle our heads between His shoulders being comforted and tranquilized by the sound of His gentle heartbeat.

Out of all the blessings that were released to the tribes of Israel by Moses, that's the blessing I choose to embrace and position myself for. This is the place I find *perfect love that casts out fear*. This is the place of security and safety through the storms of life. This is the position of the CHAIR #1 blessing Leif speaks about so often— *living from God* and not *for God*. This is the place of rest. This is the place of comfort and peace. You can live there too.

I find I must live from that place between my Father's shoulders daily. Even though I have had a significant amount of healing to my heart, mind, and emotions regarding the rejection of my father, there are still moments and situations that will bring a slight sting.

For instance, I had lunch with a friend I met a couple of years ago in Chesapeake, VA during an event at which my spiritual father, Leif, was speaking. Katrina had been adopted as a baby. She had never met her birth parents. Several years before the day of our luncheon, she had hired a service to locate her birth parents. Long story short, Katrina connected with her biological father. Not only did she connect with him at her age of forty-seven, but their relationship is also being restored (See Malachi 4:5 & 6) and they are beginning to "do life" together.

As we sat in the restaurant and she unfolded what had transpired over the previous months, I was filled with mixed emotions. She shared how they have spent time together sharing and getting to know each other.

One Sunday a situation presented itself for her to go to church with him where he's well known. He is a prominent doctor in the community he lives in. When they went to church and they walked in the building, he put his arm around her, pulled her close and then called all his friends over and said, "*I want to introduce you to my daughter, Katrina.*" She said for the first time in her life she felt like a princess, and as she related the story to me, her face showed it too. She was glowing! Her prince had swept her off her feet. Isn't this what most little girls desire from their fathers?

...the first time in her life she felt like a princess...

Katrina continued to share with me her incredible, amazing journey. There was so much going on in me as I listened to her. On the inside of me, one part was jumping with sweet joy for her, while another part of me was dealing with bitter jealousy. In my mind I was thinking, "*Why not me? Why couldn't I have experienced this?*"

It just confirmed to me what having a father present and

active in ones' life can do for them. Two years ago, Katrina was guarded and hardened, even as a Christian, raised in a Christian family. She had a very difficult time believing Father God loved her, that she was beautiful and one of His favorites. She, like many of us, just couldn't wrap her mind, heart, or emotions around that truth.

But now Katrina radiates life and intense joy! I can honestly say that she has experienced transformation. She is overflowing with excitement from receiving affirmation from a dad. In fact, his entire family has accepted her and loved her as their own. In our day, this is a rarity of a father and child relationship gone terribly wrong, being made gloriously right!

Sons Get It!

Some of us have not had healthy father role models with our biological fathers and mothers. They have not been there to reflect the true heart of Father God to us. They have not been there to unlock the door to our destiny. They have not been there to parent us from a heavenly and biblical perspective.

My insecurities and orphan mannerisms would have been heightened!

It is vitally significant for us to understand the value of having a spiritual father or mother in our lives. But do not get distracted by focusing on finding a spiritual father or mother in your life if you don't have one. Instead, let me encourage you to passionately pursue coming into a revelation and position of KNOWING your identity as Papa God's *Beloved Son* or *Daughter* first and foremost.

I believe it is crucial that we receive a transformational

revelation of our identities as a Beloved Son or Daughter of Papa God before coming under a spiritual father or mother. This isn't an absolute, but it usually works much better this way. It's a much healthier journey. I truly believe if I had become a spiritual daughter of Leif Hetland before my *Baptism of Love* that brought this revelation of a Beloved Daughter of Father God, I would have very likely put greater expectations on Leif than he could fulfill. This would have resulted in demands that would not have been realistic, as well as my insecurities and orphan mannerisms would have been heightened due to my orphan way of thinking and reasoning.

I would also encourage you not to put demands on your pastor to fill a title or position as your "spiritual father or mother" that they are not called to, or ready for. You must honor him/her as the father/mother over your church (house), and lean your heart into theirs by believing the best, praying for them, valuing them, and serving them from your position as a son or daughter of Father God. There's no way pastors can father or mother an entire congregation in most churches.

I've had many ask me what the difference is between fathering or mothering, and mentoring. Here's what it looks like to me. I believe fathering and mothering goes to a higher level than mentoring. Fathering and mothering can be much messier than mentoring, but so worth it. With mentoring, when we've had enough, we can send our mentees home. But when we're fathering and mothering, we follow through the entire process with our sons and daughters. This is comparable to our own biological children. They're in our house to stay; of course, until the day they get married or head off to college. But they're still our children. But when kids down the block come to our house to visit our kids, there's a point when it's time for them to go back to their house. See the difference?

Many times, mentors are fearful of their mentees surpassing them and they'll attempt to keep them from promotion or moving forward with their purpose and destiny. Fathers and mothers rejoice in the victories and successes of their sons and daughters. They want them to succeed. They want to pass their mantle on to their sons and daughters to assist and help fulfill their assignment. Fathers and mothers will allow their ceilings to be their sons and daughters floors.

I have spiritual sons and daughters in the United States and throughout the world. I love cheering them on! I'm so proud of them and what they're doing to expand Father's Kingdom here on earth. Hearing their testimonies and stories brings such joy to my heart. Like Beth and Jeff, my two biological children, I want to see them take the baton and run with it, going higher than I ever dreamed, and demonstrating greater signs and wonders than I've ever experienced.

Here are just a few examples of *Sons Get It* regarding alignment with Father God, as well as with spiritual fathers and mothers:

Abraham and Isaac – sons get to go into the deep places of worship with Father God, and they also receive His blessings. At times, we are uncertain what Father God might be up to, but we must trust that He knows what He is doing. As we lean into the heart of our Father, we will be better qualified to discern His heart.

I personally believe Abraham and Isaac are the perfect example of how Father God intended a father and son/daughter relationship to look like, in the natural and in the spirit.

Servants look on from a distance...sons go up with fathers! (See Genesis 22)

Joseph and Pharaoh – God ordained Joseph a father to Pharaoh (See Genesis 45:8). Fathers and sons will receive increase and save nations. As sons lean their hearts into the hearts of their fathers, they will find favor with God and man. Joseph passed the tests which qualified him to lead and oversee an entire nation, and people that weren't even his own.

Moses and Joshua – Joshua was with Moses when the glory rested on Mt. Sinai. The Glory will sustain us. Moses and Joshua were on the mountain forty days and forty nights while the seventy priests and elders looked on from a distance. Sons step into glory realms with fathers. They are released to fulfill the assignment of their fathers; they receive the promises given fathers and mothers by God (See Exodus 24:1S2, 9, 13 and 32:17).

Deborah and Barak – sons obtain victory and triumph with fathers/mothers; they will shout and rejoice together. When Barak said, "*I will not go unless you go*", I do not believe he was being a wimp as I have heard preached for many years. Deborah was "a mother to Israel." I believe he had the revelation that he needed his mother to go with him to obtain the victory (See Judges 5:7, 12, 15).

Ruth and Naomi – sons and daughters who come into

alignment with fathers/mothers will find extravagant, extreme favor, inheritance, life is restored (Ruth who loves you more than seven sons), blessings and increase. I could share many examples of divine favor I have received because of my heart being in Kingdom alignment with Father God, as well as my spiritual father, Leif Hetland. Sons and daughters live in realms of favor and increase, while workers stand gleaning of "what could be."

Ruth, a Moabite woman, gave birth to the grandfather of David. When we come into alignment with the heart of our father's/mother's, God will take us to people that are not our own, nations that are not ours, and place us in positions of authority and favor. See Ruth 1:11S13, *3:1, 18, (my daughter),* 16S 18 (where you go I will go), 2:10 (found favor in Boaz's site), 3:5 (all that you say I will do), 3:11 (a woman of excellence).

Elijah and Elisha – sons and daughters receive double portions as they pass the tests of Father/fathers, they receive the mantle that their father carries, they cross over into their destiny, and they complete the assignments given to their fathers by God. While sons and daughters experience the miraculous with their fathers/mothers, the prophets stand at a distance and observe (see I Kings 19:21, 3).

Mordecai and Esther – Mordecai was a father to Esther. Sons and daughters will step into realms of royalty together and come face-to-face with the King. Sons and daughters will have access to the King's presence, and His Kingdom. Sons and daughters will acquire favor and dwell in palaces, redeem people groups, and bring transformation to nations (see Esther 2:7, 15). While daughters dwell in intimacy with the King, concubines and maidens reside in the harem.

Paul and Timothy – Timothy was a child/son of Paul (see Acts 16:1). Timothy became Paul's companion, chosen by Paul (see I Timothy 1:2 & 18). Paul referred to Timothy as his beloved son (see Acts 19:22). Timothy **ministered** to Paul (see I Thessalonians 3:2). Paul sent out Timothy on many occasions because he had come into complete alignment with his father. Timothy carried Paul's DNA and heart, and Paul knew Timothy could be trusted with the assignment, inheritance, talents, and anointing (see I Corinthians 4:17 S my beloved and faithful child/son in the Lord). Fathers and sons redeem nations and entire people groups together.

Jesus takes His sons with Him – Jesus sent out the seventy, he had twelve disciples, but there were three (Peter, James, and John) that He personally took in close. One of them learned how to lean into Father God's heart and align his heart with His father's, that being John. Because of this leaning, John dwelled in the secret place and received the secrets of the Kingdom, secrets that men today are still trying to figure out.

Alignment For The Assignment

Sons and daughters who are in alignment with their spiritual fathers and mothers through covenant will step into greater realms of worship with them (Abraham and Isaac), will receive nations together (Joseph and Pharaoh), will ascend to new heights of Glory with fathers/mothers (Moses and Joshua), will win battles and obtain the victory (Deborah and Barak), will receive greater favor and inheritance (Naomi and Ruth), they will receive double portions (inheritance) and anointing and witness the miraculous

(Elijah and Elisha).

Sons and daughters who are in complete alignment with their father's/mother's hearts, do not stand at a distance like the servants of Abraham did, or the seventy elders and priests with Moses, or the fifty prophets around Elijah and Elisha. Sons and daughters are close-up, right smack dab in the middle of it all.

Orphans peer through windows for a visitation from Father God; sons and daughters dwell in habitation, in the secret place of the Most High!

Orphans peer through windows for a visitation.

EIGHT

LOOKING FOR THE WRONG F A T H E R

*Wherefore thou art no more a servant, but a son; and if a son,
then an heir of God through Christ.*
~ GALATIANS 4:7 ~

On The Hunt For The Missing Piece

There was such a craving in me to know what my biological father looked like. The opportunity for me to possibly find out came to me when I was seventeen years old. Like Katrina, I went on a hunt. But my efforts proved to be in vain.

A couple of my friends mentioned to me they were going over to an area in Mississippi to check out a bar they'd heard about there. Honestly, I had no interest in driving that far from New Orleans to check out a bar, but I knew my biological father lived in that vicinity. So, I decided to take the ride with them. My intentions...look him up in the local phone book, find his address, and go knock on his front door. When he came to the door I was going to say, *"Hi. I'm Leanne, your daughter, and I just wanted to know what you look like."* To my great disappointment, I couldn't find his name and address in the phone book. So, for me it was a wasted trip. If we would have had the usage of Internet and Google search back then, or one of the

I'm Leanne, your daughter, and I just wanted to know what you look like.

115

many other search engines we have today, no doubt I would have found him.

Curiosity Almost Killed The Cat

You've likely heard the expression *Curiosity Killed the Cat.* Well when I finally did meet my biological dad for the first time, and last, it almost destroyed me.

The Day The Call Came

It was spring of 1982, just before Easter, when I received the call. It was a breezy Sunday afternoon. Ray and I had just made our way into our house returning from church when the phone rang. It was my older brother, Eddie. We exchanged a minute or so of greeting, then he gave me the news, *"Faye called."* My response, *"Who's Faye?"* *"It's dad's fourth wife. She called saying he's dying and wants to see us."* I was in shock.

It was Spring of 1982, just before Easter, when I received the call.

He had received the call from Faye Crawley stating our dad had terminal cancer and wanted to see us. Wow, was that a lot to swallow.

I was twenty-six at the time. I knew God had prepared my heart, as well as my emotions, to receive this news. For two weeks prior to this phone call I had found myself unusually burdened for my biological father. I would pray and weep for him. This was so crazy to me at the time...I was praying and crying for a man I had never met, and didn't even know what he looked like. It confirms to me now that

116

it was his DNA in me, as well as a heart of intercession, which had me praying for my dad's soul.

But it still very much confused me. At times over those two weeks, I thought I was losing my mind. I wondered how I could be so broken for a man I didn't know, and had developed so much bitterness and hatred for. But God!!!

I hadn't shared the turmoil going on inside of me with anyone, not even Ray. The Friday night before the call on Sunday, we were at a fellowship for Ray's Sunday School class. After dinner, everyone gathered in the living room for a time of worship and prayer. After a time of worship the Sunday School teacher, Chris, asked, *"Is there anyone who needs prayer?"* I raised my hand and began to unfold the burden I'd had for the last two weeks, as well as the non-history with my biological father. I began to cry as I laid the facts before them. Ray was stunned by this news because he knew the years of pain I had gone through better than anyone else on earth. As usual, Ray was so very supportive.

I'm convinced if God had not laid my dad on my heart and prepared my heart with a burden for him, I would have reacted to my brother's phone call in such a way as, *"So, let him die. Who cares?"* or *"Well why do I want to go see him? He's never wanted to see me."*

Two weeks after the phone call my brother, Eddie, his wife, Joanie, and I headed toward Mississippi to see my biological father. Now, after years of tears and unanswered questions, I was going to meet the man I had always wanted to meet. Many of the questions I had would be answered, but many would not.

The entire drive there I sang over and over again in my head the song by Bill Gaither *Because He lives, I can Face Tomorrow*. The song says, *"Because He lives, I can face tomorrow, because He lives, all fear is gone, because I know He holds my future...* But I changed the word *tomorrow* to *today*. I knew that the only way I would make it through that day, that weekend, would be with my big brother, Jesus, by my side.

We drove up to my grandparents' house. I had not seen them since I was a little girl. This made the experience even more awkward. They lived on several acres and it was a long gravel driveway. We got out of the car and headed toward the side steps into their kitchen. And then, there he was, tall, grey hair, and sickly.

We drove up to my grandparent's house, whom I had not seen since I was a little girl.

He stepped up to me and placed his hands on my shoulders and said, *"You, you must be my daughter, Jill."* His wife, Faye, stepped in immediately and said, *"No honey. That's Leanne."* By this time, the cancer had gone to his brain and, well, between the cancer and the load of medication he was on, he wasn't thinking very clearly. This meant there would be no father-daughter talks on this visit, or, for that fact, no talks with him at all.

It was the strangest weekend of my life. I thought to myself, *"This happens in movies, or one reads about these types of stories in a book."* But this was no movie, and not a book I was reading. It was happening to me; it was a reality.

He was somewhat like a zombie. He was on enough medication to choke a horse. At times I would find myself looking at him and saying in my head, *"Why no letter? Why no card? Why no Christmas or birthday present? Why? Why? Why?"*

We drove home two days later. My grandparents kept us notified of his digression. Then the call came in September. He had passed away.

Awkward!

Going to my dad's funeral was probably one of the weirdest experiences of my life. In the south, we have what's called a "Wake". A Wake is held the night prior to the funeral. A Wake allows people to come and view the body and visit with the family. Visit with the family is *key* for this story.

The entire setting was extremely difficult for me. I felt as if we had driven past a random funeral home and said, *"Hey, let's stop in at that funeral home and see who died."* Everyone, for the most part, knew each other. Outside of my grandparents and my first step mom, I didn't know anyone.

My third step mom, my dad's fourth wife, had three children, all approximately my age. These three strangers were greeting all the guests, exchanging hugs and kisses, with flowing tears. I, with my two brothers, stood back and watched this scene take place for a couple of hours.

At one point in the evening I decided to venture over to the casket. As I stood looking down upon this shell of a man, I began to feel all the anger, bitterness, and resentment well up inside of me. Thank God, my first step mom, Bobby, who was present at the funeral, intercepted this wave of emotions.

Bobby was my dad's second wife. She came into our lives while my older brother was stationed out in California at Camp Pendleton during his basic training with the Marines. Bobby and her husband invited me out for a summer visit to their home in Del Mar Beach, CA. I was *twelve* years old at the time. I wasn't too sure of the idea, but Bobby, living two blocks from the beach, definitely peaked my interest. I love the water and beaches, and I've been on some of the most beautiful beaches of the world.

There are three significant memories I have of my time at Bobby's home that summer. One was I met my stepbrother, Mark, and stepsister, Jill, while I was there. They were at their mom's house for the summer. I always wanted a sister, so this brief time with Jill was cool.

There was another event that took place while visiting Bobby that literally almost took my life. Remember I was *twelve* years old. I was down at the ocean with Mark and Jill swimming. I was a little too far out and got caught up in an undertow. I tried to break free of it, but it continued to drag me out from the shore farther and farther. I just knew I was going to die. Finally, the lifeguard on duty must have spotted my dilemma and had to come to my rescue. This event scared the "you know what" out of me. But it didn't keep me from the beauty of the ocean. I go to the oceans of the world every chance I get.

And the final experience I had while visiting Bobby is clearer to me today than any of the rest. For some reason, I walked into Bobby's bedroom one day. Bobby was on the phone with someone. Then Bobby said, "*Would you like to speak with her?*" and handed me the phone. This would be the only conversation I would ever have with my biological father.

When I put the phone to my ear, nervous as all get out, I said, *"Hello."* He returned with, *"Hi, how are you? This is your dad."* I retorted, *"Yeah."* Then over the next minute or so I really do not remember any exchange of conversation, but he did the talking. Finally, he said, *"Well maybe when you return to Louisiana we could get together and see each other."* To this day, I said something I've always regretted. I said, *"I don't think so. I have a dad (Claude). You've not wanted to have anything to do with me until now, why would I want to see you?"* and I handed the phone back to Bobby and walked out of her bedroom.

I wanted to see this man, my dad, more than anything in the world. This is what I was almost consumed with over the previous six years, seeing the man face-to-face that helped bring me into this world. But I wasn't going to give him the opportunity to hurt me again. I was not going to give him the right to see me when he hadn't been there for me the last *twelve* years.

> *I wanted to see this man more than anything in the world.*

There Are Good Fathers Out There!

Let me take a side road with you for a moment. I want to state there **are** fathers out there that have been prevented in one way or another from having the opportunity to be the *dad* to their children that they longed to be. Here's Todd's story:

It was in late spring of 1992 in Charleston, S.C., when

a very difficult chapter in my life was ending. The closing sentence was being written as I drove away. As I pulled away from the curb, I could see my five-year old son in the rear-view mirror of my car, waving goodbye, as he was being held by his mom on the side of the road. However, this wasn't an ordinary goodbye, it was a final goodbye. Not only was I waving goodbye to my son, I was also saying goodbye to a seven-year marriage that had somehow gone terribly wrong. For the sake of everyone involved and for my own sanity, I was headed back home for moral support and a chance to begin the next phase of my life.

As I pulled away, the guilt and fear that overcame me was almost paralyzing. The enemy was yelling in my ear, "You're a failure!" The truth was, I had been a good dad and a good provider. I loved my son with all my heart and he was the apple of my eye. I'm sure the only thing that kept me from stopping and turning around was the grace of my Father God and the assurance that I was doing the right thing. There was also the knowledge that I had done my very best and it just wasn't going to work. I had learned a very important life lesson through this very painful time in my life: you can't make anyone love you!

Thank God mom and dad had taken our family to church. I had accepted Christ into my heart when I was only nine years old, and I had been baptized in the Holy Spirit when I was fourteen. However, just because you grow up in church doesn't mean that you've got it all together when it comes to living a successful Christian life. I had certainly been taught the right way, I just hadn't done too well when it came to abiding by the rules. I was too busy "sowing my wild oats."

After high school, I worked and attended a local college, but it seemed my life was going nowhere. I finally woke up and decided that I didn't want to work at the local shoe store all my life. There's only so far you can climb on the "corporate ladder" selling shoes. So, I decided to visit the local Navy recruiter. My dad had been in the Navy, so I thought it would be a good idea to follow his lead and get out of town to go and make something out of my life. I did well on the placement exam and was placed into the Naval Nuclear Program. Little did I know what awaited this young man who had once sold shoes for a living. Anchors away!

The nuclear program was very challenging—two years of college level courses in only six months. I would go to school early in the morning and would finally make it home late most nights. My nose was stuck in the books on the weekends, as well. Reason being, if you didn't pass "Nuc" school, you were immediately sent out to the fleet. I wasn't too keen about that idea. So, I decided to work very hard...failing was not an option.

Prior to attending Nuclear Power School, I married a young girl I had dated in high school. As you can imagine, the first year or so of our marriage was rocky.

Unfortunately, she would be home at our little efficiency apartment most days all by herself. By the time, I finished school at night, I was too tired to be a good husband. This caused a lot of conflict between us, but I didn't have an answer to the problem. Unfortunately, this is one of the reasons why the divorce rate is so high in the military.

I made it through Nuclear Power School and was headed to upstate New York to tackle the next phase of my training. I completed that portion of my training with flying colors and was sent to the Portsmouth Naval Shipyard for my first duty assignment—a submarine by the name of USS Simon Bolivar, SSBN 641. This is where the story gets interesting. The same God that I had known in my youth, resurfaced again. It's true, if you "Train up a child in the way he should go, he will not depart from it."

While on my first duty assignment, I made another life-changing decision. I'll never forget looking out the second-floor window of our cottage in Maine. It was in the early spring of '87, as the snow was beginning to melt, when I recommitted my life to Christ. However, this time it was different. I was older and more mature and understood the commitment I was making. The decision I made on that early spring day totally transformed my life and I have never been the same.

I caught the fire and began witnessing to anyone who would listen about what God had done in my life. The

Holy Spirit was so evident in my life that everyone around me began to take notice, to the point that the Leading Petty Officer of our crew asked me if I would consider being the Protestant Lay Minister onboard the submarine. I had no clue what he was talking about, but it didn't matter, if it meant doing something for God. I did understand the term "minister." Little did I know that this was going to be my first assignment for the Kingdom. Another life lesson, "If you're faithful in the little, God will make you ruler of much."

During my time in New England, my first and only son was born, a handsome young man by the name of Michael. Man, was I on top of the world. I'll never forget holding him up in my arms and dedicating him to the Lord. I have dedicated a lot of babies since that time, but this was my first and most important one. I was performing the duties of a pastor and hadn't even been commissioned by the Lord yet. By the way, his mom had already had him dedicated at the local Catholic Church. But remember, I was the Protestant Lay Minister.

Michael was growing and maturing into toddlerhood; all the while his mom and I were growing farther apart. My love for God continued to grow, but it wasn't the same in my marriage. Unfortunately, she began to resent my relationship with the Lord, ridiculing me for praying, attending church and reading my bible. I was called names like, "Christian fanatic" and "holy roller." She insisted that I stop attending church and start partying with her. The crazy thing is that partying had never been a part of our relationship. I believe it was the enemy's tactic to keep me from moving forward into my designed destiny. He was drawing the line by bringing division between my wife and me.

It got worse. I awoke one night to Michael crying by my bedside, wanting to know where his mom was. I found her outside, talking to the guy across the street. He was single, in the Navy, "needing someone to talk to." I was told, "We are just friends." Isn't that the way it always begins? The next several months were "hell on earth" with sleepless nights, hospital visits due to anxiety attacks, paranoia, suspicion, lies, and phone calls at work accusing my wife of running around on me.

It all came to a head one afternoon after praying to my Father God and asking him to show me what was going on. I was at my wits end and needed to know the truth. The Holy Spirit immediately compelled me to pick up the phone and call the "guy across the street." I thought I would just outright ask him what was going on between him and my wife. I didn't have the chance to say a word. He answered the phone, and thinking I was one of his friends, immediately began to tell me that he was "in love with the girl across the street." In the process of him telling me this, he also began playing his answering machine and I heard my wife tell him that she loved him, as well. Wow! It's true, be careful what you pray for. Father God had shown me exactly what I needed to know.

The following months were very difficult, to say the least...filled with the pain of rejection. I finally decided to move out of our home, leaving it for her and my son to live in. She and the "guy across the street" continued to have a relationship, so we eventually got a divorce. And after eight years of faithful service to the Navy, I received an honorable discharge. What a journey it had been...from selling shoes to sailing a ship.

Before you feel too sorry for me, remember how Father God causes all things to work for our good, even the painful ones? He truly does redeem and restore all that the enemy has stolen.

I made it back home on that late spring day of '92. Shortly thereafter I met the girl of my dreams. We fell in love and after twenty years of marriage we have three beautiful girls of our own. I was called to preach in 1996, at thirty-three years of age. Today, we co-pastor a successful ministry of twelve years.

I wish I could share a "fairy tale" ending when it comes to my relationship with Michael, but I can't. His mom eventually married the "guy across the street." They also went through a divorce after only one year of a very tumultuous marriage. She and Michael, along with her current husband, now live in a town about one hundred miles from where I currently live.

I fervently pursued a relationship with Michael after his mom and I had gotten a divorce. My wife and I would drive ten hours every other weekend just to get him and spend time with him. Thank God, his mom eventually started meeting us halfway. I religiously paid child support, as well as financially helping him get through college. I did everything that a part-time dad can do. However, his mom's attitude towards my commitment to Christ continued to surface over the years and eventually began to affect my relationship with Michael. It seemed that she would have done anything possible just to keep him away from the influence of my family and me by keeping him busy with sports and other events on the weekends. It became a battle just for the opportunity to see him.

I received a phone call from Michael several years ago. He seemed a little broken as he began to tell me what had happened. It seems that while over at a girlfriend's house, the Lord had dropped a scripture in his spirit. He then asked his girlfriend if he could borrow a bible. Unfortunately, he knew very little about the Word of God.

The scripture was 1 Corinthians 9:16, "For though I preach the gospel, I have nothing to glory of: for necessity is laid upon me; yea, woe is unto me, if I preach not the gospel!" I think it's fairly obvious that the Lord has placed a call on Michael's life to preach the gospel. By the way, baby dedications do work! He has since graduated college and works at a local grocery store near his home. Our family only gets to visit with him a couple of times each year, but we continue to pray for him.

There are those times that I feel the heart of our Father God. He has these wonderful children whom He has given life to, yet He doesn't get to enjoy a relationship with much of them. However, I'm thankful He hasn't given up on any of us. Even though I still don't have a very good relationship with my son, I haven't given up on him either. Just know, not all part-time dads are deadbeats.

I'll never forget the words that Michael said to me after I had picked him up from the babysitters when he was about four years old, "Daddy, I love you as big as the sky!" Daddy God, "I love You as big as the sky!

I have wondered more times than I can count what would have happened that day if I would have said to my dad, *"Yes, I'd love to do that!"* or *"Ok, let's get together."* I wonder if it would have really happened. Would he have followed through? If so, how would my life have been different today?

The Wake and Funeral

Now back to the Wake. I'm sure Bobby had witnessed the pain and hurt in her own two children, Mark and Jill, over the years, so she was tuned into what I was going through standing at his casket. I was literally about to jerk his corpse up out of that casket when Bobby came over to me, put her arm around my waist, and gently ushered me off to a side area. Bobby was not a Christian, but as a mother she knew how to love on me and comfort me. I'm thankful to this day that Bobby was there for me.

The next day was the funeral. Another extremely awkward situation. Here we were, the three of us kids, sitting with the rest of his family in the area reserved for "FAMILY." This FAMILY section was very visible to everyone present. As everyone else was seated facing the casket, there were several rows off to the left-hand side up front, so our right sides were to the guests. I could almost hear the voices in their heads, *"So, who are those three sitting up there? You see them, the girl with the blonde hair and the two guys."* I was so thankful when the funeral was over.

The best memory I have of his funeral was Bobby arranged for the three of us, along with Mark and Jill, to get together in a hotel room for a few hours to talk and share our lives. To my disappointment this would be the first and only time this would happen.

We headed home afterwards thankful that it was all over with, so I thought. It was the following February when I received my inheritance in the mail. I wasn't sure what my inheritance would look like, but I knew I would receive something significant since my dad was retired from the Navy and owned his own business. To my understanding, he was quite comfortable.

$1.00

I opened the envelope and pulled out the check. I was utterly shocked. I had received my inheritance of $1.00. In the memo, it had "Estate of Edwin Crawley." I was fuming! In the state of Mississippi, the law says all you have to leave is $1.00 to your heirs. So, each of the five of us received $1.00, except for Mark, he also received our dad's watch.

Well, I majorly reacted. I hired an attorney to try and fight for my inheritance. It was said to us that we were originally in his Will for a rightful inheritance. But his wife told him if he didn't change his Will and give us just the $1.00, then she would not take care of him in his last days. I'm not sure if this is true, but I do know all we got was the $1.00. His wife and her children received *my* inheritance.

I did hire an attorney and began to fight hard. But as the months went by, I noticed I was becoming very sick. My body ached and I had other symptoms that brought concern. My mom and my older brother would tell me, *"Leanne, let this go. It's destroying you."* But no way, if I couldn't have my dad in my life, then I wanted his money.

One day I had gone to the doctor and as I was sitting in the waiting room I noticed a magazine sitting on the table. Something on the cover caught my attention, the word *Depression*. I picked up the magazine and began to read the inside article on *Depression*. As I read the symptoms of *Depression*, I realized that was me. It hit me like a lead balloon. How could this happen to me, I was a Christian? I had the revelation this was not what God would want me to do, or how He would want me to live. I immediately dropped the pursuit of my inheritance, and not surprisingly, my medical condition improved almost immediately.

Needless to say, I did not run to the bank and cash my $1.00 check as soon as I received it. In fact, I hung on to that check for approximately twenty-three years. I laminated it and used it multiple times when I would teach on *Forgiveness*. During our years with Teen Challenge, I taught the class on *Growing Through Forgiveness*. It was a five-day class. Each student who came through the program had to take that class twice. I would use that check, in the midst of my teaching, to share how I got free from the *cancerous spirit* of *Unforgiveness*.

How I got free from the cancerous spirit of unforgiveness.

Unforgiveness will rot away our souls. *Unforgiveness* has three close cousins – *bitterness, anger, and resentment*. Before walking through the painful process of forgiving my biological father in September 1984, I was camping out with all of these life-threatening enemies.

Up until September 1984 when I chose to forgive my biological father, I was being controlled by him, even though he was not in my life. It was as if he had a chain around me and by his actions was leading me through life. I had allowed his actions and attitude to dictate my actions and attitude. This scenario affected many people in my life. At times, it was as if I was carrying a bag of garbage around with me. I think you'd agree with me that not many people want to hang out at a garbage dumpster. Now I'm sure anyone that knew me at that time would tell you I wasn't a bad person. But like so many of us, I had my ways that would damage and injure relationships because of the garbage I carried around with me regarding my *fatherlessness.*

But on that night in September 1984 when I made the extremely, difficult decision to forgive my dad, the chain that he had around me was broken and the garbage bag I had been carrying around with me for years disappeared. I was free!

When I would speak on *Unforgiveness* in any given setting, I would dramatize this illustration to my audience. I would take a rope and tie it around the waste of someone who would represent my dad. Then I'd tie the other end around my waste. I would have a plastic bag literally filled with garbage and toss it over my shoulder. Then I'd have the person representing my dad begin walking around the room, minding his own business, making his way through life. He would drag my mind, emotions, and feelings around with him, many times controlling them, his actions and attitudes dictating mine. And along the way my garbage was bumping into those I came in contact with. Then as I would forgive my dad, I'd untie the rope, drop the garbage bag, and go on with my life, free to be who my Papa God created me to be. It was very effective and worked every time.

NINE

MY INHERITANCE

And he shall go before him in the spirit
and power of Elias,
to turn the hearts of Fathers to the children,
and the disobedient to the wisdom of the just;
to make ready a people prepared for the Lord.
~ LUKE 1:17 ~

Receiving Mantles For Ministry

The very few times I heard my paternal grandpa (my grandma would refer to him as *Crawley*) preach, enthralled me. He was a Baptist preacher and always preached *fire and brimstone* messages. Back then, those were the type of messages we thought were the holiest of holiest messages.

I regret that I didn't get the opportunity to spend more time with my grandpa, than with his son, my biological father. The times I got to be with Grandpa were some of the most precious memories I have, though they were few and far between. I could sit and listen to his stories for hours. I remember the few times my brothers and I would go for a weekend or a school holiday break to visit my grandpa and grandma. We would be so excited for this opportunity.

They lived in the country, opposed to where we lived in a

suburban neighborhood. As typical back then, they lived in the parsonage next door to the church, and across the street would be the cemetery for the local town. On Saturday, we would help my grandpa clean the church in preparation for Sunday service.

In 1997, I heard Father God speak very clearly to me. He said, *"Leanne, because your father refused the mantle from his father for declaring the Gospel throughout the world, it has been passed on to you."* At that point, I began to understand much more about the burden I had had in my heart for the lost and discipling the nations of the world (See Matthew 28:19). At times I would think I was going mad when such an intense burden would well up in me for those without Jesus. I would receive messages to preach, but had no platform to preach them from. I would cry out to God asking why He would give them to me, when I had no one to preach them to. I have folders of messages that just now I'm able to pull out from the archives I've had them stored in.

Clearly back to the time of my salvation in 1976, I would receive downloads for messages and sermons, but it just didn't fit. I was a woman, and women preaching, in that era, was almost unheard of. I would cry out to God, *"Why are you doing this? Why didn't you create me a man? Men can preach these messages, a woman can't."* Little did I know the journey my Papa God had waiting for me.

Propelled into My Designed Destiny

I'm amazed at how Father has our lives in order and *works ALL things together for our good.* I believe there are greater levels we move to during our lives, as well as new seasons. Much of the time, those seasons prepare us for the new levels.

I recently experienced a new, higher level towards fulfilling my *Designed Destiny*. It's hard to explain, but I will try my best.

On March 8, 2012, I was overseeing GMA's resource table at a conference in Houston, Texas honoring the legacy of Papa Jack Taylor. It was the day after my birthday. As we were sitting in the evening service where Bill Johnson was speaking, I received a text message from my daughter. In her message, she told me that my eighty-two-year-old mom had fallen and was in the hospital. We began texting back and forth as she related to me what had taken place. She had broken her femur and it was serious.

As much as I wanted to hear what Bill was saying, at that point he lost my attention and all I could think of was my mom. I excused myself through the people sitting down the row and headed to the foyer to make some calls.

As the days passed by, my mom grew worse. The hospital staff told us that if anything took her life, it wouldn't be her broken femur. But due to her being immobile, the likely hood of pneumonia setting in or some other complication, that would take her life. On March 30th my mom entered heaven due to pneumonia. It was such a bitter/sweet moment to experience this prayer warrior, that prayed daily for her children and grandchildren, receive her upgrade.

My mom gave her life to Jesus in the mid-seventies. Like me, this would be a decision that would totally impact her life. She knew she was called to prayer, especially for her children and grandchildren. She would always have her prayer list right inside her Bible.

My mom had a hard life. She was the youngest of six; the five older were all boys. There were several years between the youngest son and her. Her mom died when she was at a young age from Parkinson's disease, as did her father. Her father's death was much more tragic.

My mom's dad had had a stroke and was basically immobile on one side of his body. He was a smoker. One day he was sitting on the side of his bed trying to refuel his lighter. Back then they didn't have *Bic* lighters. They used lighters that had a screw in the bottom. Lighters were refillable. One had to unscrew the screw, take a small lighter fuel can and pour the liquid into the hole in the lighter. You then replaced the screw and it was once again ready for use.

Due to his partial paralysis, he had to maneuver filling the lighter with one hand. On this day, he was holding a lighted cigarette between his lips. Someway the fuel was ignited from the cigarette and he was engulfed in flames, which took his life.

Because of an early death of both of her parents, her five older brothers raised her. My mom outlived all five of her brothers, losing two to alcoholism, one choking to death in a steak house just a few days before Christmas, and the other two dying from natural causes. Over the years my mom became a tough woman due to the many hard-knocks she was dealt throughout her life.

I had the honor and privilege of presenting the eulogy at my mom's funeral. People were laughing one minute and crying the next as I told stories about this amazing woman. She made an impact on so many peoples' lives. Even though my mom was tough on the inside, she was beautiful on the outside. She had purchased a new outfit, all red, for Easter. It was gorgeous. She had not gotten to wear it for Easter, so this is what we buried her in. She looked beautiful with her silver hair all in place.

I will never forget how stunning she looked as long as I live.

I will never forget how stunning she looked as long as I live.

I miss my mom terribly, but I'm comforted by the fact that she is having a holy blast dancing in heaven on streets of gold. I told her shortly before she received her upgrade, *"Mom, I'll see you in heaven."* I look forward to that day when she and I will dance together for our King of Glory.

My God-Ordained Inheritance

The day after my mom's home going I went for a walk in the park next door to our house. I was grieving her loss, but was processing the news I had just received that the small amount of inheritance my mom had planned for my four brothers and me was taken from us just three months before her death, at no fault to my mom at all.

As I was walking through the park with my iPod and headphones listening to worship music that was ministering to my heart and emotions, I cried out to my Dad. *"I don't understand."* I told Him, *"My first inheritance was taken from me, now my second opportunity for an inheritance has been taken from me, as well. Why?"* Then He spoke!

Within 30 minutes my heart was still and knowing Him.

Just like Jesus did against the storm on the sea, when my Father speaks, any and every storm within me comes to a halt. He spoke so

139

gently to me and said, *"My daughter, Leanne, just remember that your inheritance is not the riches of this world, but the nations of the earth."* (See Psalm 2:8) Well that's all I needed, and within thirty minutes my heart was *still and knowing Him*. I was at peace and rest.

About four days later my Father spoke to me again. This time He said, *"My daughter, I know I told you your inheritance is not the riches of this world. But just like with Abraham, Isaac, and Jacob, I will also bless you with the riches of this world."* I must tell you, since that moment my husband and I have witnessed this promise from my Father begin to take place. We are being blessed in every area of our lives. We have such a good Papa!

The Blessing Of A Legacy

My mom might not have left me an inheritance, but she left me something greater, and that's a legacy. I mentioned earlier that she worked for the airlines. In fact, she began working for Eastern Airlines in the late fifties, eventually moving on to National Airlines and retiring from Pan American. Many times, as we traveled to various cities and nations during my growing up years, I would pay attention to how my mom would handle various situations. I'm convinced that even way back then, I was in an apprenticeship school learning the ins and outs of international traveling. Since 1987 I have overseen well over seventy-five international ministry teams. I know I was created to help introduce Father's heart for the peoples and nations of the world to His children. My mom, unknowing to her and to me at the time, helped prepare me for this assignment.

Since my mom's upgrade, there has been a major shift that has taken place in my life. As I said, it's hard to explain. What I feel

Holy Spirit has ministered to me is likened to when the mantle of Elijah fell on Elisha at Elijah's upgrade into heaven. Before that moment, Elisha was not fully released to fulfill his *Designed Destiny*. Now, as he received Elijah's mantle, his entire life took a major Kingdom shift. With his father gone, he went forth with what he was created to do. I feel that way. There has been a supernatural shift in my life since my mom's upgrade.

Servantship Or Sonship?

I know that I'm doing what I was created to do. It's so much easier now as I do it from the revelation and position as a daughter, instead of a servant. Servants wait in line to receive a paycheck. Sons and daughters receive inheritance. I'd much rather receive an inheritance any day than a paycheck.

To clarify, I do serve...God and others. But I serve from who I am, not for what I want to be. I serve as a daughter from love. A servant works! Sons and daughters serve. I serve because I want to, not because I feel I have to in order to gain approval or acceptance.

I serve from who I am, not who I want to be.

I went from seeing myself as a servant to a daughter. Servanthood is not wrong, but there's a higher place we can live from. We are to serve from our positions as sons and daughters. We do not nullify being servants of God, but there is a higher level ... Sonship!

Our Kingdom Affirmation

For years and years I strived to be a woman of God. We bring people to Christ and begin working to make them men and women of God. I believe we've done the *sons and daughters of God* an injustice by not allowing people to embrace and walk out their identity as sons and daughters of a loving Father.

When Jesus was baptized by John the Baptist in the Jordan River, and His Father's voice was heard from heaven, God didn't say, *"This is my beloved savior...my beloved Messiah...my beloved miracle worker in whom I'm well pleased."* He said, *"This is my beloved **son** in whom I'm well pleased.* Jesus was baptized with water and with power from the Holy Spirit. But more than that I believe He received a *Baptism of Love* from His Father. He was anointed by Holy Spirit, and affirmed by His Father.

Whose Are You?

It is so critical that we have a revelation of this. This Kingdom revelation will bring transformation to our lives. We must know who we are and *Whose* we are. We must embrace our true identity as sons and daughters of a loving Father, or we will struggle with our identity every single day of our lives. As in the story of my spiritual daughter, Sonia:

> *I grew up as a Baptist preacher's kid hearing about God. I knew Him as "Our Father, who art in heaven..." but never understood He was actually MY Father right where I was at! He has carried me through many disappointments, heartaches, and struggles all the*

while remaining in His embrace. Several years ago, in Houston, Texas while attending a conference with Leif Hetland and Leanne Goff, God began solidifying my identity as His redeemed daughter.

In April 2010 I was diagnosed with Multiple Sclerosis. I remember being given the news and admitted to the hospital for the first dose of intravenous steroid treatments and many, many MRIs. While I was in the hospital Papa God gave, me Psalm 27:1`6 and He began showing me I was now His healed, redeemed daughter!

In May I was reconnected with an old high school boyfriend after twenty years. He was recovering from brain surgery he had in April due to seizures he had been having since shortly after high school. Once we began talking, my feelings for him began to evolve quickly and deepen. Neither him nor I had ever married and I was beginning to think that God had saved us for each other. The doors of my heart had flung wide open to him because of the healing that Papa God had brought to my heart from abuse as a child. I had never trusted a man until then, and now I trusted him so deeply and true.

Exactly one year after we reconnected I moved back to the town he lived in with the intentions of us getting married. We were married in July 2011 with everyone's blessings. Our wedding was like a high school reunion with people celebrating our union as husband and wife. Everyone wondered what had taken us so long.

Shortly after we were married things began to change. He stopped valuing me as his wife, and his material possessions became more important, i.e. cars, engines, tires, etc. I was having trouble with MS and was taking medication to cope with some of the symptoms and pain I was experiencing. He quit a job where we had very good benefits to work for his brother where we had no benefits. The intimacy between us came to an abrupt stop and it was as if we were just "living together." The commitment for life we had made before God and witnesses was shortly lived. He became very controlling, as well as emotionally abusive, and to a point, physically abusive. He never hit me; although there were times he would grab me hard to where he would leave bruises. One night we had just arrived home and we began to argue in the car. He got out and pulled me from the passenger seat by my hair and threw me to the ground jumping on top of me holding me down. A neighbor from across the street came outside to see if I needed any help.

In the midst of this, instead of going to God and crying out to Him, I began to drink. I drank because I wanted a "quick fix" to the situation and I didn't think God would "fix" it quick enough. The worthlessness I began to feel as a wife began to make me feel inadequate as a woman, and drinking alcohol caused me not to feel or think about reality. The combination of the alcohol and the medication I was taking for MS made the entire situation more volatile. Twice my husband locked me out of our house and changed the locks. My answer to his behavior was to drink.

The first time he locked me out of the house was on Thanksgiving; the second was on February 10, 2012. After the second time, I decided enough was enough! I couldn't live this way any longer and I needed to find the place I had gotten off track and get back on it. I needed to get my heart and mind back to where it belonged—with Papa God!!! I told my husband I was going away for a few weeks (since he had changed the locks on me, I couldn't go back to him) and I left to stay with my spiritual mom and dad, Ray and Leanne Goff, in Alabama.

On February 28 I received a call from my husband telling me he wanted a divorce and that I had complicated his life! I was so angry and again all I wanted was a "quick fix." I headed out in my car with the purpose of getting drunk and forgetting. On my way home, after several drinks, I got lost. It was dark and it had been raining all evening. I called Leanne to see if maybe they could help me find my way to their house. They told me to look for landmarks around me. I hung up and began looking around. When I looked to the road all I saw was red. A car was stopped in front of me at a 7`-point stoplight. I rammed right into the back of them. The impact pushed their car twenty to *thirty feet through the intersection to the other side. Miraculously no other cars were at this intersection at the time. Though their car was damaged in the back, it was drivable. Mine was completely totaled.*

I was arrested that night and placed in lockdown for thirty days. In the car, I hit was a couple with her ninety-two-year-old mother in the back seat. The woman and her mother were both transported to the hospital and released the next day, but because there were injuries I was now being charged with two felony counts of assault. Each count carried two to twenty years in prison.

April 2012 was exactly one year since I had left my secure job, my nice apartment and car, good medical insurance and relocated to be with my fiancé. It was exactly a year since I had been looking forward to a married life with my husband and our own home. One year later I had just gotten out of a thirty-day lockdown jail stint, I had no job, no car, no house, no insurance, no husband, AND facing four to forty years in prison! Two months later I was served with divorce papers.

I was set for pre-trial on October 16, 2012 with a trial date of October 29th. With everything mounting up against me, the stress and weight were too much for my body and I had a relapse of MS the beginning of October. I was admitted to the hospital for another round of intravenous steroids.

In the midst of this huge storm, one thing remained constant and true for me—my Papa God and being in His loving arms. There was not anything I had done or could ever do that would catch Him off guard. Nothing I could do or ever do that would take His love away from me. He had given me His perfect peace. A peace that was all mine. A peace that surpassed all understanding. If I took my eyes off that peace, all the worry, stress and confusion would come rushing in and lay me flat! I knew Papa would take care of me, though I was extremely scared at times. Whenever I would experience fear I would go to my secret place with Him and He would hold me in His lap and just ask that I trust Him as my Papa. I was learning a new facet of my relationship with Him. It wasn't a "quick fix" for sure, but it was a sure fix!

During this entire time people from all over the world were praying for me. Some close friends, some people I had just met, as well as a few I had never met. They prayed for favor over my life and that God's face would shine favor on me and He would be my light.

On October 16, 2012, I went to pre-trial. Up until this time, the District Attorney had not even wanted to discuss my case. He was pushing for a minimum of twenty years in prison and wouldn't listen to any offer of a bargain from my attorney. He wanted to use me as an example.

After the docket call the lawyers and the Assistant

District Attorney went to the back to discuss the cases. My lawyer came back and said the DA wanted to talk with her about my case, but he was in a trial. She told me to go on home and she would call me after she talked with him. On my way home, she called and said that, unbelievably, the DA wanted to offer me a deal of a year of drug court. The deal was...I had to find one in the county I resided in, or I would have to go back to Alabama and attend one there. My lawyer was completely surprised by this. I was ecstatic to take the offer! I thought God had answered my prayer, but my Daddy wasn't done yet.

I found a drug court program and called my lawyer. She informed me that county was not accepting any applications at the time. In the meantime, the victims in my case had a meeting with the DA and the Victim's Advocate. As soon as they walked in they asked the DA how they could help me. How THEY could help ME!!!!! They wanted me to come up with a plan that would help what took place on February 28th to never happen again. Plus, they wanted to meet me. I came up with a plan with the help of my spiritual mom, Leanne. The victims accepted it and set a date for me to meet them.

On November 27, 2012, I met with the couple I had run into that dark night many months before in February. Almost exactly nine months later I finally had the opportunity to ask their forgiveness for what I had done and share my heart with them. To my utter surprise this meeting wasn't about me.

The man began to tell me that he understood exactly what I was going through, and that he had been where I was. He had been an alcoholic and God had used AA in his life to help him deal with issues instead of turning to alcohol. He has had a closer walk with God because of it and gives Him the honor and glory. Then his wife spoke.

She, too, knew the devastations of alcohol. She had been an alcoholic, as well. She began to tell me her story. Fifteen years ago, her first husband had died and her world fell apart. Six months after his death, on what would have been his birthday, she had gone to the cemetery drunk and had taken a bottle of Schnapps with her for him. As she was leaving the cemetery driving down the road, she saw headlights coming her way. She swerved, but so did the other car, which resulted in a head-on collision.

There were three people in the other car, a grandmother, a mother, and a six-month-old baby. The grandmother and six-month-old baby were killed on impact. The woman was sentenced to fifteen years in prison, serving only six months. She said she promised the mother of the baby that she would never drink and drive again, and testified she has kept that promise. Now she was asking the same of me. She said all she wanted was to help one person; to help them not have to go through what she went through.

That person was me! She told me I was one of the first people she had ever told her story to. She wanted to help me because the same thing could have easily happened to me! As it turned out, I am the same age she was when this happened to her fifteen years ago. Upon leaving that meeting she came up to me and gave me a big hug.

I am not being charged with those two counts of felonies anymore. I have been extended mercy! Isn't God sovereign? Who else could've orchestrated something like this? My Papa, that's who!

Throughout the last three years Papa God has been establishing my identity in Him. I am His beloved and He is mine! I am His dream! He dreamed me into existence and that dream became a reality the day I was born! Throughout this journey, I have become my Papa's FAVORED, HEALED, REDEEMED daughter! Oh by the way, I've been healed of Multiple Sclerosis too! No lesions and no trace of any! I have a good, loving, and wonderful Daddy!

I believe when Holy Spirit led Jesus into the wilderness, He went through the test of Sonship. What did Satan say to Jesus? *"If you are the Son of God..."* Jesus' identity was tested. Satan did not say, *"If you are the Messiah...the Savior...the miracle worker...the deliverer."* Jesus had to be one hundred percent secure in His identity as a son to fully accomplish His assignment. Like Jesus, each of us must also be secure in our identities as sons and daughters of our loving Father to fulfill our *Designed Destiny* from our *Master*

Designer.

I lived too many years as a woman of God, striving, performing for my Father's love and acceptance. I knew, to an extent, that He loved me. My thinking was that He had to. I mean...He created me. He was Father...but *my* Father! Now I love living from my identity as a little girl with a big Dad. Kids have more energy, and let's face it, usually more fun.

Supernatural Transformation

I am no longer satisfied with a little touch from God or a change; I want to continuously be transformed by His powerful love. That's what I experienced with my *Baptism of Love* in October 2003. Those who know me have witnessed the transformation in my life.

I am no longer satisfied with a little touch from God or a change.

Let me give you my illustration of transformation. If I have a paper clip and stick it in an electrical outlet, I will get a strong zap, I will give a shout and my fingertips will possibly be black. But, say I was to go outside my home, climb up a utility pole, and wrap my arms around a transformer at the top of that pole. I guarantee you I would be transformed. I would NOT look the same anymore, inside and out! I would talk different. I would walk different. I would live different!

This is what takes place when we allow our Father to wrap His arms around us and ours around Him...we will be transformed! Just like an encounter with an electrical transformer will inevitably bring a complete transformation, so will an encounter with our God and His extravagant love.

Leanne Goff

TEN

THE ENEMY NEVER RELENTS

*And he brought up Hadassah, that is, Esther, his uncle's daughter:
for she had neither father nor mother, and the maid was fair and
beautiful; whom Mordecai, when her father and mother were dead,
took for his own daughter.*
~ ESTHER 2:7 ~

The Day My Body Crashed

June 22, 2010 the enemy made another attempt to stop me in my
tracks. On June 21, I was feeling great and living life to its fullest. The
next day I woke up barely able to take a shower without being totally
exhausted. This went on for days. I kept telling my husband,
"*Something's terribly wrong.*" Honestly, I thought I was losing my
mind.

Prior to June 22, 2010 I was riding my outdoor bike almost
daily, doing up to one hundred stomach crunches on my abs coaster,
and living a very active lifestyle. Then it was if, overnight, someone
took a straight pin and popped a balloon, sucking all the air and life
from me. After one month and a battery of tests, I was diagnosed
with severe Adrenal Fatigue.

I can remember sitting on the couch in my living room for two
to three hours at a time, looking out the window with no life in me

wondering, *"Is this what it's like when someone is on the threshold of dying?"* Not that I had any pain, but just no strength, energy, or life in me to function. For me to go into the kitchen and make a sandwich would totally exhaust me. I would become overwhelmed with the thought of getting in the car and going to the grocery store. I remember times when I would go to the store with Ray and I'd have to hold on to the handle of the shopping cart because I was so exhausted. There were other times when after only twenty minutes in the store I'd say to Ray, *"We need to leave. I need to go home."*

Of the nine symptoms of Adrenal Fatigue, I had eight of them. The only one I did not have was insomnia. In fact, all I wanted to do was sleep. To get up in the morning took everything in me, and then I'd need to sit on the couch for a while before I could go on to the next thing. Sometimes it would be one or two in the afternoon before I could muster up enough strength to take a shower. Those that know me know I am a multi-task person with a high A personality. But during this dreadful period of my life, I had challenges concentrating and communicating and would become overwhelmed and anxious at the slightest thing.

There are three levels of Adrenal Fatigue – mild, moderate and severe. My case was severe!

Symptoms of Adrenal Fatigue:

- Difficulty getting out of bed in the morning
- Non-refreshing sleep
- Ongoing fatigue not relieved by sleep
- Weariness
- Lack of energy

- Lethargy
- Inability to handle everyday stress
- Feeling overwhelmed by relatively minor challenges
- Mild depression
- Struggling to get through the day
- Tendency to avoid conflict
- Mental fogginess
- Fuzzy thinking
- Frequent infections
- Longer recovery times from illness, injury, or trauma
- Low libido
- Increased cravings for salty foods, sugary foods, refined carbohydrates
- Caffeine dependence
- Lightheadedness
- Low blood pressure
- Intolerance to cold
- Hair loss

Causes of Adrenal Fatigue:

- Alternating Shift Work (improper sleeping schedule)
- Disease
- Death of Close Friend or Family Member
- Drug or Alcohol Abuse (organ abuse)
- Head Trauma
- Loss of Job
- Moving to a New Place Alone
- Relationship Issues
- Serious Burns (Even Severe Sunburn)
- Severe Emotional Trauma (Death or Being the Caregiver

of a Sick Individual)
- Sickness
- Steroid Drugs and Type Two Diabetes (which is an Adrenal Issue)
- Stress
- Work Situation
- Lack of proper nutrition

I remember one difficult trip I made. GMA was holding a conference at a church in Chesapeake, VA the August following my crash. I headed to Virginia a couple of days before the event to make sure all was in order. This would be the first traveling I had done by myself since my crash.

This would be the first traveling I had done by myself since my crash.

I flew from Huntsville, AL to Atlanta, GA before flying onto Virginia. My plane departed Huntsville late causing me to miss my connection in Atlanta. When the tires of the plane touched down in Atlanta, I turned on my cell phone so I could call the person picking me up in Virginia to notify them that I wouldn't be in at the scheduled time. To my disappointment my cell phone had no charge.

Now here I was with no phone and having to get my flight rescheduled. I took care of the flight, then headed to a Delta Sky Club Lounge to charge up my phone and find a place to rest for a few minutes. When I walked into the Sky Club Lounge of the terminal I was in, it was packed with people, with literally nowhere to sit. I became overwhelmed with the situation and could feel the tears welling up in my eyes. I was tired and exhausted already, but knew I needed to find a place to land my body for a rest.

I turned around, left that Sky Club Lounge and journeyed on the tram over to another terminal hoping to find a place of abode. I finally arrived at another Sky Club Lounge that was sparse with people. I sat down, quickly pulled out my cell phone and hooked it up to an electrical outlet. The first person I called was my husband and I began to sob on the phone to him. I said, *"Ray, what is wrong with me? I go all over the world, even to Pakistan by myself, and I can't even make it to Virginia!"* As he always has, Ray began to love on me, encourage me, and pray for me. I got my composure and received strength through his prayer and was able to move forward.

Before my crash, I didn't know where my adrenal glands were,

They are of extreme importance to our bodies and lives.

much less what their function was. But I quickly became educated. I could probably write my own book on these little almond-sized organs that can wreak havoc in our lives if not maintained and taken great care of. I have learned they are of extreme importance to our bodies and lives.

The adrenal glands are tiny organs that rest on top of each kidney. Despite their small size, the adrenal glands play an important role in our bodies, producing numerous hormones that impact our development and growth, affect our ability to deal with stress, and help to regulate kidney function. We derive much of our energy from these organs, thus where we get the term *adrenaline*.

Because the hormones released from the adrenal glands are so important to the overall functioning of our bodies, adrenal disorders can have serious consequences on our health, even causing death.

The adrenal glands and the thyroid glands are at the opposite end of the same stick. When the adrenal glands are depleted, the thyroid gland will kick in and begin to work overtime, thus many people are diagnosed with hypothyroidism, when, in actuality, their adrenal glands can be the real issue.

Individuals from all areas of life, every culture, all ages and every race can suffer from adrenal fatigue. Adrenal fatigue occurs when the activity of the adrenal glands diminishes. The less function that is going on in the adrenal glands, the more organs and systems in the body are affected. Changes occur in carbohydrate, protein and fat metabolism, fluid and electrolyte balance, heart and cardiovascular system, as well as sex drive.

What Saved My Life!

My doctors, as well as my nutritionist, told me it would take a minimum of three to four months to rebuild my adrenal glands and get them back to a healthy state.

Like many others, I've spoken to who have experienced Adrenal Fatigue, doctors wanted to put me on antidepressants. I did not feel that was an option for me, so I decided to call my nutritionist, Jim Hangstefer, for an all-natural antidepressant. When I told Jim about my situation, he immediately responded, *"Leanne, I have just what you need and I promise it will help you and you will start to feel a difference almost immediately!"* I did, not due to antidepressants, but all-natural supplements.

Through many people praying for me globally, accompanied with the supplements I was taking, I gained new strength every day.

I learned how to listen to my body and give it what it needs. I continue to learn more about rest and how critical it is to our well-being. I'm learning how to set boundaries in an entire new way and say, "**No.**" I've learned that we only have one body, and after it's gone, there isn't another one this side of heaven.

When my body first crashed and I had no clue what was going on, I told Father, *"I don't know what's going on in my body, but I want to get every nutrient out of this situation that I can."*

I know I have not completed the assignment I was put on this earth to complete, and I want to run the race well, and finish it. I also realized this was another one of those times the enemy tried to distract me and bring my life to a standstill.

There are still times when I feel my oil gauge running low and I need to pull back, listen to my body, rest, and *"Be still and know He is God"* (See Psalm 46:10). It is interesting. Most of us take great strides to keep our automobiles maintained and in great condition, i.e. alignments, oil changes, tire pressure, etc., but when it comes to our health, we don't do nearly as much to keep our bodies maintained and kept up.

The Launching Of A Blog Site

God has shown me that He has put the sword of Goliath in my hands to do vengeance against the enemy. Like David, I'm called to cut off the enemy's head and destroy this device that he has used against so many of God's precious children. I have had emails, calls, as well as Facebook messages from many who are going through much of what I have gone through. I've had the opportunity to encourage them, give them hope, and suggestions to help them to be on their way to wellness.

I've had women contact me who have been dealing with this for years, have lost their jobs, and have had to move in with family members because they can barely get out of bed in the morning. I know of great men and women of God, pastors, preachers, and evangelists, who have also severely crashed. They've had to learn what Leif calls *"the hard work of rest"* through their illness. One such minister, who witnesses profound miracles of healing in his meetings, asked God after his crash, *"Father, why didn't you just supernaturally heal me?"* He said Father responded, *"Because son, I wanted you to learn a lesson from this. You cannot continue to live like you've lived."*

Let me be one hundred percent clear, our loving Father does not invoke this type of sickness upon His children. In fact, I don't believe any sickness is from our Father, no more than I'd want any of my children to be inflicted with a disease or illness. I love them too much to see them suffer in any way, and my love for my children pales greatly in comparison to the love our heavenly Father has for us.

I am so grateful to my Heavenly Papa who loved me enough to slow me down, to be still, to know Him, and for bringing people into my life to help me and love me in a time of great need. My amazing husband, Ray, stayed by my side all the way through my crash, washing clothes, cleaning, waiting on me, cooking, and loving me through the entire process.

My immediate family, as well as my spiritual family, came to the side of Ray and me and helped cook, clean, and just be there for us in whatever we needed.

Multitudes prayed for me around the world when at times I wasn't sure I'd make it, but I did!

ELEVEN

WILDERNESS TESTINGS

The LORD thy God in the midst of thee is
mighty; he will save, he will rejoice over thee
with joy; he will rest in his love, he will joy
over thee with singing.
~ ZEPHANIAH 3:17 ~

A Diamond In The Rough

Wilderness experiences have groomed my life for what I am doing today. There is a love relationship with our Father that develops in our wilderness times. In Song of Solomon 8:5, Jesus is referred to as "*Beloved,*" but in Deuteronomy 33:12, **we** are called "*Beloved.*" Our wilderness seasons can cause our hearts to lean into one another. We will also come to experience and understand the *goodness* of Father God in order to demonstrate His Kingdom here on earth. The wilderness times will bring out the precious jewel we were created to be for our Father.

In Matthew 17:5, on the Mount of Transfiguration, God declares, "*This is my beloved Son, in whom I am well pleased.*" This is the second time Father affirms His *Beloved* Son (See Matthew 3:17). Jesus wasn't just God's Son; He was His *Beloved* Son! There was a leaning of hearts together between Father God and His Son.

Scripture says, *"And Jesus being full of the Holy Ghost returned from Jordan, and was led by the Spirit into the wilderness."* (Luke 4:1) It goes on to say that after Jesus' testing in the wilderness, He came out in the power of the Spirit (See Luke 4:14). Jesus was baptized with water, baptized with Holy Spirit, and finally received His *Baptism of Love* when His Father declared over Him, *"This is my beloved Son, who I am well pleased with."* Jesus' testing in the wilderness was a testing of His identity, **Sonship**.

Most of us have been baptized in water. Many of us have been baptized in Holy Spirit, but few of us have received our *Baptism of Love*. This is where our identities as sons and daughters are sealed. Like Jesus, if we do not live from our identities as sons and daughters of a loving Father, we will not be entrusted with our inheritance here on earth. Our very identity will also be tested. The enemy will come and say to us, as well, *"If you are a son? If you are a daughter..."*

This is where our identities as sons and daughters are sealed.

How does it feel to walk in our identities as sons and daughters? How can we live from that position? Jesus grew in the Lord with His earthly parents who took care of Him. Jesus knew His Father and His place in His Father's heart. The nature of the enemy is to question the Word of the Lord. Could it be that the word he used with Jesus is pivotal to *Sonship*?

It was the will of Father for His Son, Jesus, to be tempted by the devil. Sometimes Father allows storms to come our way for us to be equipped to face them, then what is inside of us comes out.

Sonship!

It was clear that the enemy's point of temptation was about Sonship. He will throw questions, confusion, and condemnation on this one thing—Sonship. He will question God's love for us, our integrity before our Father, the Word of God, His intentions for us, and the intentions of our hearts. There are, and will be, seasons of wilderness times where we will be led into temptation. The measure of our understanding on Sonship is what will give us the ability to come out conquering. This is part of our training for reigning. Both David and Jesus were trained in the wilderness, as well as many other great men and women of God in the Bible. Their training prepared them for promotion, and equipped them to reign with authority for the Kingdom of God.

When Father speaks, everything is settled. But when He is quiet, sometimes things are just too hard to face. When He is silent about our circumstances, let us hold on to what He has spoken in the past. Don't let those seasons of prophetic words burn just one time and get fired up just for a moment. Those are sparks, which later become fires, that we need to carry and to let them burn, especially in times when we are alone, discouraged, disillusioned, and tired. Jesus said man should live by every Word that proceeds from the mouth of God. When we are tempted, and are being questioned on our Sonship, we must go back to what Papa has spoken over us. What we did cannot mess up His plan. So, let's not wallow in the corner. Stand up, go back, and be refreshed from His Word!

The enemy works by deception. He speaks the war of words! The devil will do everything to question who Father is to us, and who we are to Him. Let it be settled that we are a beloved son or a beloved daughter of God, and that He *is* well pleased with us.

Looking For A Home

One of my primary assignments is partnering with my spiritual father, Leif Hetland in reaching the 1.5 billion Muslims who have yet to experience true love. These 1.5 billion Muslims are trying to find their way back home. They're looking for their Father. They are the Ishmaels who have been cast out into the desert to survive on their own, unwanted, wandering through life looking for a home.

In many ways I can understand how a Muslim must feel, or better yet, what Ishmael must have felt like. No, I wasn't literally kicked out into the desert to live and fend for myself. I'm sure it must have gone through Ishmael's head a thousand times over, *"Why has my father done this to me? Why am I an outcast? I never asked for this. I didn't do anything wrong."* Ishmael was rejected and abandoned by his father, and really left to die.

> *Ishmael was abandoned and rejected by his father, and really left to die.*

Like Ishmael there are so many children that have been rejected, abandoned, or abused by their father. This has affected their entire life and many of them live from a paradigm that our God is the same way. He's mean, abusive, distant, or as I thought for many years, He created me, but didn't have time for me. Yes, that's how I viewed God. He was a Father because *the Bible told me so*, as we sang in Sunday School or Vacation Bible School when I was a little girl. He tolerated me, but didn't celebrate me. He had more important things to do than spend time with me. I sang it because *the Bible told me so*, but I didn't believe it.

I viewed God as this superior being sitting high up on His throne holding a rod in His hand with dry-ice-smoke hovering all around Him. I knew He was just waiting for me to get out of line or do something wrong, and then He would take His rod and hit me over the head with it to straighten me out. I envisioned God as Creator, Ruler, Judge, Disciplinarian—He was GOD!

What person wants to spend time with a being like that? Who wants to hang out doing *quiet time* with someone who you feel really doesn't have time for you, or really doesn't want to be around you? There are scores of Christians that view God like this. I talk with them every day. Many of those Christians want Jesus to return for them so they can get away from the circumstances of this world, not to be with their loving Father in heaven. I believe that most Christians don't even think they'll see God when they get to heaven. Oh, they'll see Jesus walking the streets of gold and they'll bow down and worship Him for eternity. But God will be off in some big back room taking care of the affairs of this world, dealing with rebellious, wicked countries, sending down tsunamis and category five hurricanes to chastise them.

This picture of God is so terribly wrong and distorted. I believe God totally intended for our biological fathers to live and demonstrate to their children what the true heart of Father God is like—loving, caring, protective, joyful, good, hopeful, and always there when you need Him. But the truth is this has not been the case. So many of us had a father that was distant, selfish, bad, untrusting, and never, or almost never, around when we need him.

So many of us had a father that was distance.

The *#*#*#

During my ten years with Teen Challenge, I sat with many men and women, whether in my office or in a prison, and I would ask them, *"Tell me about your father."* or *"Where's your father?"* Most the time I'd receive a reaction somewhat like, *"The *#*#*#. I have no idea where he is."* Or, *"I hope the *#*#*# is dead somewhere."* Or, *"Who cares! the *#*#*#."*

I've come to understand the difference between a person who has been nurtured, protected, and valued by a loving father, and one who hasn't. For the person who didn't have a father that was there for them no matter what, who was loving, protective, and valued them, this person either didn't want to have anything to do with God, or very little to do with Him.

For those that had a father who demonstrated the heart of God as being One who is loving, caring, protective, wants to spend time with them, and is always there for them, this person was generally strong in their faith and commitment to the Kingdom of God. Those people didn't have nearly the life-issues to deal with as those whose father was absent from their lives, or abusive.

There are also those whose father was present in their lives, but was *out to lunch* so to speak, i.e. hid behind the newspaper, escaped life with the TV when they were home, a workaholic, or consumed with golf or some other sport or recreation that came before their children.

Papa's Sons And Daughters Are Coming Home

Malachi 4:5 & 6 states, *"Behold, I will send you Elijah the prophet before the coming of the great and dreadful day of the LORD: And he shall turn the heart of the fathers to the children, and the heart of the children to their fathers, lest I come and smite the earth with a curse."*

I believe we are entering the season where fathers' hearts are turning toward their children, and the children are responding to this invitation. Like in the story of Katrina, her heart is relating to her father's, and together they will do great things for the Kingdom of God. If one can put a thousand to flight, just think what two can do (See Deuteronomy 32:30).

I believe that we are entering the season where father's hearts are turning toward their children.

We were created for God's Glory, *"For I reckon that the sufferings of this present time are not worthy to be compared with the glory which shall be revealed in us. For the earnest expectation of the creature waiteth for the manifestation of the sons of God"* (Romans 8:18S19).

Did you get that? We were not only created for our Father's Glory, we are His glory.

If you have been abandoned and/or rejected by your earthly father (or mother), your Father in heaven wants you to know how much He loves you, adores you, and is always available to you. He is attracted to you and you are very valuable to Him. As much as you desire to be in His presence, He longs to be in your presence. You are His little girl/little boy, and He is your big Papa. He finds you extravagantly beautiful, and as He has told me many times—He has your back!!!

TWELVE

FATHER GOD IS TRUE!

(Additional Testimonies)

He that hath received his testimony
hath set to his seal that God is true.
~JOHN 3:33~

Sandy

When I was in fourth grade, my parents called me into their bedroom and handed me an envelope with a flower drawn on the outside. Inside this beautiful envelope was a life-altering letter. Inside, handwritten words shared why my skin was "darker than everyone else in the family." The letter revealed the man I had known as "Dad," was not my biological father. They offered no further explanation. I was too young to realize I needed to know more.

Looking back, I recognize many lies that crept into my life after this news was revealed. Things like...I didn't belong and I was unwanted. I never asked who was my father? What nationality am I? Do I have siblings? What is his name? Does he even know if I exist? To this day these questions have never been answered. It never occurred to me to ask these questions until I was fifteen years old.

I was attending a Youth Convention in New Orleans. When I called home, my mother shared with me that New Orleans was the place of my conception. I remember getting off the pay phone and looking at the men passing by and wondering, "Is that my father?" I intently looked to see if anyone resembled my coloring. I am dark skinned, dark hair, and have deep brown eyes. My mother was very fair skinned, blonde hair, and blue eyed. That conversation from the pay phone put me on a quest to find my biological father.

During my childhood, my mother struggled with alcohol and drugs to numb the pain of death in her life. When I was in kindergarten my seven-month-old sister died. We all grieved for our loss, but my mom was consumed with losing her. I remember wanting to be with my mom, but she had locked the door and said she was having a "spell." I remember thinking "But I'm still here even though my sister is gone." At Christmas time three years later, our family faced another tragedy. We had a house fire and lost everything except, literally, the clothes on our backs. The final breaking point for my mother was the death of her mother, and then the death of her stepfather to cancer. When she couldn't bear the pain anymore, she tried committing suicide. She had attempted a few times until, finally, she was put in a psychiatric ward. She was diagnosed with manic depression and bi-polar. To further compound my feelings of abandonment, my mom and stepdad got a divorce during this season.

My teen years were tumultuous at home. I wanted nothing to do with my mother since she wanted to die. I decided she would be dead to me because of all the pain she had caused. So, I escaped the yelling, fighting, conflict, and drunkenness by hanging out at my friends' homes. Several of these families were Christian homes.

I received Jesus as my Savior a few days before my twelfth birthday. I was blessed to see families interact and enjoy and share life with each other. However, in my home I learned to wear masks. I believed no one cared how I felt or what I thought. I was frequently corrected by my mother and father, and told that what I thought and felt was wrong.

In high school I was well liked. I was voted to homecoming court my senior year, and later to Prom Queen. Even though I was smiling on the outside doing the royalty wave from the car, I was devastatingly broken on the inside. All the activities and success in high school were not celebrated by my parents. It was rare for them to attend any of my activities.

During my senior year of high school my mother moved out of our house and dated a man for a couple of months. My mother had met him at AA and became pregnant with twins at the age of thirty-seven. This was a turning point in our relationship. I had asked for forgiveness for my part in this rocky relationship, and God began restoring it. When I was eighteen, instead of hatred towards my mother, I was sad for her challenges that lay ahead. I wanted to be helpful and was excited to have twin sisters. I always wanted another sister and I was getting two!

On September 23, 1995, my high school sweetheart and I visited my mother and sisters to show her my engagement ring. We hugged. She was so excited for me and my bright future of being married to a doctor. During this visit with my mom I had an incredible idea! I asked her to draw a picture of what my biological father looked like. My mother was a highly-gifted artist. One of the many creative art pieces she had done was a self-portrait. She had also drawn pictures of me. It would be easy for her to create this picture because she was so talented! So, she agreed to draw a picture of my father for me, but that opportunity never took place.

On September 25, 1995 I received a call at four o'clock in the morning from my step dad. He said he needed to come over and talk to me. I asked who was hurt, but he wouldn't answer me. My step dad said my mom had died in a car fire a few hours earlier. My very first thought in the midst of overwhelming sorrow that brought me to my knees was, "I will never find out who my biological father is!"

I had lost my mother, father, and sisters, and in a moment, I was orphaned. I had lived a life with an orphan mindset for years, but now it was suddenly validated. This mindset was only compounded in the season following her death by never having a revelation of a Father's love for me to begin with.

The autopsy revealed she didn't die by accident or the fire. She died of blunt force trauma to the head. Someone had murdered my mom, placed her body in her car, and ignited it to make it look like an accident. I spent the next year being a detective, trying to bring closure to something that only God could do for me. To this day her homicide is an unsolved cold case.

After the death of my mother, I continued with my wedding and marriage. My fiancé and I had a rough relationship. Looking back, I was more in love with his family than him. I began to shut my friends out and only hang out with him. I liked how controlling he was because it made me feel like someone wanted and cared about me. When I married him I was hoping to **finally** belong. I loved his family. They played games, they laughed, and they enjoyed each other. I wanted so badly to belong to a healthy family. I knew his controlling nature was bad, but I was desperate to finally have a "healthy" family, so I married him despite knowing I would probably regret it for the rest of my life.

We moved from our home state of Iowa to Oklahoma in 1999. Abandonment became more of an issue for me when he traveled a lot and because I was away from his parents. Because of my pain and immaturity, I threatened to leave the relationship while he was out of town. So, in the crazy cycle we called marriage, he left a threatening voicemail saying he was on a ledge of a building and going to jump. My past wounds and pain of my mom's failed attempts of suicide flooded me. I realized there wasn't real love in the marriage. So, I was done. I flipped a switch and wanted no more pain, rejection, or abandonment. I quickly divorced him.

During this time God brought a woman, Marian, into my life with the ability to love me unconditionally. She was like a mother figure to me and she made a profound effect on how I saw God. She taught me about the Holy Spirit as a person who comforted me and would never leave me. She was God's love in action to me. She would share how God's love never fails and shared stories of His goodness. This was the beginning of learning my Father's true heart towards me.

I would arrive at her house a mess and leave refreshed and excited for what God had for me. She made such a huge impact on my life that I would later name my daughter after her. The idea that God was good had been very foreign to me. Religious people told me that what happened to my mom was God's will. Well, I didn't want a God who would do that to me, be mean, and teach me a lesson. I saw God as callous and thought I should just be thankful He doesn't kill me on the spot! Marian had introduced me to the true nature of God and challenged everything I had thought was true about God.

I stayed in Oklahoma and made a life for myself by creating a successful small business. I also met and married a fantastic man. I knew from the beginning he would be an incredible father to our children. He has shown our three children and me what a father should be like. He is loving, caring, and protective over us.

Even though I had a step dad who was there since my birth, it has always felt like he fathered me out of obligation. I am thankful for what he did give me, but I needed more than what he was capable of giving me. I felt guilty for wanting more so I stuffed the feelings down deep. In all this I was barely beginning to understand that Father God knew I existed, and that He loved and cared for me. I never had a person of flesh and blood that was fatherly to me, to speak life over me, to encourage me, to support me, to care about what I thought, or even say that I was special.

On a recent international trip with Global Mission Awareness, Father God began to reveal Himself to me in a way I had only dreamed about. All the talk during the trip of spiritual sons, daughters, mothers, and fathers was extremely strange to me, to say the least.

I met a couple, senior to me, on the team named Betty and Rene who were like two lovebirds. They were full of joy and life like I had never seen before. One day Rene asked me where I came from. I thought, good question! I'd sure like to know that myself! I had asked and been asked this question my ENTIRE life. I told him my story and God deposited a father's heart of love for me in Rene in those moments. From that point on, when I would see Rene and Betty in the *morning at breakfast, he would always comment in a sweet fatherly way how beautiful I looked and he would just love on me.*

During a special time of communion Rene ran to me and said, "My daughter, my daughter" and professed his father's heart towards me. Immediately I struggled with this new fatherly-type of love I was experiencing. I was thinking he was just saying that to be nice, or because he felt bad for me. It was at this time that a friend showed me I had believed a lie that I didn't belong. This lie was even affecting my life with my three kids and husband, and I didn't know it. I realized that I would frequently withdraw from my family because it felt like I didn't belong! The Lord resolved that lie in me right then and there.

Rene continues to be kind and affectionate towards me, as if I was his own little girl. Father God is showing me how much he loved me through this man. He was the flesh and blood to be a conduit of my Father's heart toward me. It took these kind and gentle words from a physical, fatherly man that set me up to understand how Father God saw me! I didn't know how powerful words could be until Rene spoke them to me. His words brought life and healing to the dead places in my heart. The void of a Father's love has been filled in my life. I am finally able to receive from my Father God!

Rene'

I was born on Mother's Day in Havana, Cuba May 12, 1946. I almost died at birth. Soon after birth my mother had a nervous breakdown. She needed to go away to recover. As a child I was very introverted, shy, timid, and fearful. I went to LaSalle Catholic School. During retreats I would experience the presence of God. These were times of ecstasy and deep communion with the Lord. I could not move, talk, or respond to the environment as I was filled with His presence.

Little did I suspect that my life would go into a path of destruction. One of my family's characteristics was that of professionalism. My mother was a physician and my father an attorney. Several of my aunts and uncles were also physicians and attorneys. Every Sunday my family would meet. It was an incredible potpourri of worldly knowledge and wisdom. A character that was above all others was my maternal grandfather, Juan Bautista Kouri, a professor of medicine at the University of Havana. He was a remarkable physician, surgeon, and an innovator in medicine. He was also a Grade 33 Freemason.

I know that generational curses affected me. The years I lived in Cuba between 1946`1960 were very dry, spiritual years. Overall there was ungodliness in my family, as I would also say in most families at that time. Holy Spirit had not fallen in the Catholic Church yet. We did not talk about Jesus, nor did we have a Bible.

When I was about twelve or thirteen years old, a Catholic brother expelled me from the LaSalle chorus for naively laughing with my peers about a foolish situation. I felt hurt, rejected, and humiliated. I went outside the school to get an ice cream. The vendor not only gave me the ice cream, but he also gave me a pornographic booklet. The moment I saw those pictures and read the booklet, a demon of lust came into my life and affected me for over forty years.

It did not help that at the same time I received "growth injections" that greatly stimulated my sexuality. My first emotional sexual romantic love relationship was with a prostitute when I was thirteen years old. Love became totally contaminated with sex. Sex tried to fill a bottomless place of hurt. I became a sex addict. I lived with feelings of rejection, abandonment, shame, insecurity, fear, worthlessness, self-pity, self-hate, etc. There were many strongholds that needed to be destroyed, such as shame and fear.

In 1960 I came to Miami, FL at the age of fourteen. Depression hit me really hard. I began to drink alcohol to relieve the pain. In 1970, I realized I needed to find God and receive healing. At that time, I connected to a Hindu Guru and began intense meditation practices to seek the presence of God.

By the grace of God, I went to medical school and trained at the University of Miami for seven years. I completed trainings in internal medicine and nephrology.

By 1982 I had a dialysis unit and a large practice of medicine and nephrology. I was in my second marriage and had a second child. Rapidly I became totally addicted to cocaine and lost everything. I left Miami and went to a treatment center in Mississippi by the name of Copac. There I suffered the worst feelings, moods, and emotions. The self-hate was intense and consumed me. The sense of grief, regret, and loss overwhelmed me

I had lost my wife, my daughter, my house, and my practice of medicine. I was under the control of total cravings and obsessions. I was convinced that I could never recover and I was planning my next relapse, thinking that surely, I would die. I had no other alternative. I felt totally hopeless.

That day I walked into the woods and found a small pond. I could not take it any longer and asked God to please kill me. I was totally broken down, and fell weeping into the humid earth. A new idea came into my mind. I said to God that if He did not want to kill me, to please take all the negativity, cravings, and hell that were inside of me "Whosoever shall call on the name of the Lord he shall be delivered." (Joel 2:32)

Suddenly, a gust of wind came. I heard the sound of the leaves being shaken, the waters of the pond were stirred, and in a moment God took away all that was killing me. He absolutely took away the cocaine addiction, the cravings, the self-hate, the depression, the negativity, and the darkness. I was filled with light, love, joy, peace, beauty, clarity, and happiness. It was an event that I still clearly remember. I never used any drugs again. God sovereignly healed my cocaine addiction in one moment in 1983.

As I went back to the housing complex, I began to declare of how God can heal addiction in an instant. They thought that I had taken drugs, so they did a urine test on me and the results were negative. I kept telling people that God healed me at a pond in the woods. I called it God's pond.

I stayed an entire year in Mississippi. I went to Alcoholics Anonymous, did The Twelve Steps, had a sponsor, and confessed my sins in a Catholic Church. The drug addiction was totally over, but the issues of relationships, love, sex, and deep hurt, were not healed. I brought my two children to Mississippi because I knew that they had been deeply hurt. But they were young and rejected any therapy. I renewed my efforts to find the God that had healed me.

I talked to priests and ministers from different denominations, but then went on in a more profound way into esoteric spiritual psychologies, the new age, Buddhism, Hinduism, eastern and native American practices, etc.

By the year 2000 I was losing hope of finding God and being healed. I had three marriages, three divorces, and multiple relationships. I would ask myself "Why do my soul mates become hate mates?" I even called it as Freud called it, "repetition compulsion in hell."

No amount of therapy, religion, spirituality, meditation, mantra, etc. healed my relationship problems. I also had two very hurt children, and tons of negative feelings in me.

I had two sisters, Maria and Fifi, who were always praying for my salvation. In 2001, my mother had triple coronary bypass surgery. Postoperatively she had severe gastrointestinal bleeding that would not stop. My mother was bleeding to death. I saw my sister Maria placing her hands on my mother's belly and making strange loud noises. The bleeding immediately stopped.

I felt the power of God in the room and was very impressed. I liked it. It was the first time that I saw the manifest power of God in a Christian. I did not know that nice Catholic women would do such things. I saw Jesus healing my mother. In that vision Jesus said to me, "I am happy that you are here." Later I wept. I was being touched by the kingdom of God, by the King himself. I was witnessing the healing power of God...Love in action!

My mother recovered from the coronary bypass surgery, as well as the postoperative bleeding and was able to go home. Later that year she went to glory with the Lord. We had a Catholic *charismatic mass as part of the wake presided by father Dan Doyle. Maria, my sister, invited everybody to do the prayer of salvation. I thought to myself, "I have done all kinds of prayers, and today I am going to say this prayer." So, I repented of my sins and accepted Jesus as my Lord and Savior at my mother's funeral. The most important event in my life took place that day.*

The same thing that happened to me in Mississippi, in which I was healed from my cocaine addiction, happened again twenty years later at that mass. This time it was a profound deep healing of all the things that I worked so hard to heal from for so many years. The Light that came into me created will, discernment, boundaries, wisdom, and discrimination. At that moment, I was healed of sexual addiction and old woundings. I knew this God that came into me in Mississippi in 1983, and then again in 2003, is the one true God! I cried for a long time, grieving, and trying to understand why it took me such a long time to find Jesus. The father of lies blinds and deceives (See 2 Corinthians 4:4).

For three months, I underwent daily intense deliverance. Every morning Holy Ghost would take me to a place, in which I had to repent, renounce, forgive, and cast out demons in the name of Jesus.

I am a new Christian, ten years now, but many Bible verses rapidly took root in me. Tears of joy and gratitude flow from my eyes. He is about miracles, wonders, grace, and mercy. His love is fathomless and is available to all. He who is forgiven much, loves much. My life was a search for healing, and healing came, Jesus came.

Soon after my salvation I began training at Christian Healing Ministries under Francis and Judith MacNutt. I built a prayer room in my house in which there is ongoing salvation, healing, deliverance, prophetic, and intercession services.

My two children were very hurt. I accepted my mistakes and how I had hurt them. God had forgiven me. I asked my children for their forgiveness. The Lord of miracles is always doing miracles. He imparted to me the spirit of fatherhood, something that was never in me. My son told me, "This is the first time that you are a father."

The Lord has also given me many spiritual children to protect and guide. They are such a joy. My practice of medicine has become a healing and revival center of the Holy Spirit. Every day of my life I see miracles of salvation, healing, and deliverance. The Kingdom of God is manifesting in my office.

The years of besetting major sin that separated me from God and caused havoc in my life have ended. I can choose blessings today. I want your love, Lord. I want to love you more. I want to visit your throne. You said ask and you shall receive.

My Father is joyfully waiting for us. He wants to candidly converse with us. This is the day of love. There is love going back and forth between you and your Father. Be filled. Relax. Let go. Explode. Be in the language of love.

I am open and vulnerable like a little child who's learning how to walk, running to hug my Father, running to my Father without any agendas. There is nothing in my heart; there is nothing in my mind. I am running, tumbling, falling, getting up, happy, happy, happy, free, without any agendas, just running to hug my Father. I melt in the arms of my Father. This earthen vessel rests and the spirit soars. My Spirit is full of Holy Ghost.

EPILOGUE

FATHER'S LOVE LETTER

My Child,

You may not know me,
but I know everything about you.
Psalm 139:1

I know when you sit down and when you rise.
Psalm 139:2

I am familiar with all your ways.
Psalm 139:3

Even the very hairs on your head are numbered.
Matthew 10:29-31

For you were made in my image.
Genesis 1:27

In me you live and move and have your being.
Acts 17:28

For you are my offspring.
Acts 17:28

I knew you even before you were conceived.
Jeremiah 1:4S5

I chose you when I planned creation.
Ephesians 1:11-12

You were not a mistake,
for all your days are written in my book.
Psalm 139:15-16

I determined the exact time of your birth and where you would live.
Acts 17:26

You are fearfully and wonderfully made.
Psalm 139:14

I knit you together in your mother's womb.
Psalm 139:13

And brought you forth on the day you were born.
Psalm 71:6

I have been misrepresented by those who don't know me.
John 8:41-44

I am not distant and angry,
but am the complete expression of love.
1 John 4:16

And it is my desire to lavish my love on you.
1 John 3:1

Simply because you are my child
and I am your Father.
1 John 3:1

I offer you more than your earthly father ever could.
Matthew 7:11

For I am the perfect father.
Matthew 5:48

Every good gift that you receive comes from my hand.
James 1:17

For I am your provider and I meet all your needs.
Matthew 6:31-33

My plan for your future has always been filled with hope.
Jeremiah 29:11

Because I love you with an everlasting love.
Jeremiah 31:3

My thoughts toward you are countless as the sand on the seashore.
Psalms 139:17-18

And I rejoice over you with singing.
Zephaniah 3:17

I will never stop doing good to you.
Jeremiah 32:40

For you are my treasured possession.
Exodus 19:5

I desire to establish you with all my heart and all my soul.
Jeremiah 32:41

And I want to show you great and marvelous things.
Jeremiah 33:3

If you seek me with all your heart, you will find me.
Deuteronomy 4:29

Delight in me and I will give you the desires of your heart.
Psalm 37:4

For it is I who gave you those desires.
Philippians 2:13

I am able to do more for you than you could possibly imagine.
Ephesians 3:20

For I am your greatest encourager.
2 Thessalonians 2:16-17

I am also the Father who comforts you in all your troubles.
2 Corinthians 1:3-4

When you are brokenhearted, I am close to you.
Psalm 34:18

As a shepherd carries a lamb,
I have carried you close to my heart.
Isaiah 40:11

One day I will wipe away every tear from your eyes.
Revelation 21:3-4

And I'll take away all the pain you have suffered on this earth.
Revelation 21:3-4

I am your Father, and I love you even as I love my son, Jesus.
John 17:23

For in Jesus, my love for you is revealed.
John 17:26

He is the exact representation of my being.
Hebrews 1:3

He came to demonstrate that I am for you, not against you.
Romans 8:31

And to tell you that I am not counting your sins.
2 Corinthians 5:18-19

Jesus died so that you and I could be reconciled.
2 Corinthians 5:18-19

His death was the ultimate expression of my love for you.
1 John 4:10

I gave up everything I loved that I might gain your love.
Romans 8:31-32

If you receive the gift of my son Jesus, you receive me.
1 John 2:23

And nothing will ever separate you from my love again.
Romans 8:38-39

Come home and I'll throw the biggest party heaven has ever seen.
Luke 15:7

I have always been Father, and will always be Father.
Ephesians 3:14-15

My question is... Will you be my child?
John 1:12-13

I am waiting for you.
Luke 15:11-32

Love, Your Dad Almighty God

ADDITIONAL THOUGHTS

 Lucifer was the first orphan! The ultimate spiritual orphan!

Orphans want everyone around them to be miserable just like them.

 Orphans are greedy. They want it all for themselves.

 Satan's job description is to get us thinking as orphans, not knowing we are loved, accepted, and deeply valued by our Wonderful Father God.

 Orphans compete for a place of recognition, position, and power.

 Orphans "think" they are homeless and cut off from God and His love. This causes orphans to replace intimacy with shame and fear. It doesn't say, "*For God so tolerated the world*", but "*God so loved the world*".

 Orphans feel "tolerated"; sons and daughters know they are loved.

 Orphan thinking begins with you to doubting Father's love, kindness, and generosity towards you. Then you quickly begin to doubt the love of others around you, including family.

We are to be like God our Father. He made us in His image.

 We sin willfully and through orphan thinking. Adam and Eve had a home, but after choosing the way of sin, they were homeless.

 Orphan thinking will deteriorate relationships (Genesis 3:11-12).

 Orphan thinking will separate us from Father God, as well as others.

 "I will not leave you as orphans, I will come to you" (John 14:18)

 We can either live in a spirit of Sonship, or an orphan spirit.

 The Church is a global orphanage.

 Many of us are fatherless people born in a reproduction camp.

 God could have referred to Himself as a Heavenly Boss, but He's our Heavenly Father.

LEANNEGOFF
MINISTRIES

MINISTRY CONTACT INFORMATION:

Leanne Goff

info@leannegoffministries.org

For more information on upcoming conferences,

International Vision Trips,

or to purchase items from our web store,

please visit our website at:

www.leannegoffministries.org

PO Box 681

Newark, OH 43058

361.652.3529

ADDITIONAL RESOURCES BY LEANNE GOFF

A Journey To Your Identity—Book

Leanne uses the introduction of this message by Leif Hetland, her spiritual father, as a springboard to show us the value and importance of leaning our hearts into the heart of Father God, as well as spiritual fathers and mothers. When we lean back into their hearts and come into alignment, we will receive the secrets of the Kingdom, as John the Beloved did, and go forth in our assignment and fulfill our destiny.

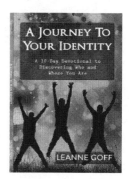

Experiencing Papa God's Transforming Love – CD

In this message Leanne shares how after many years of successful ministry, she found herself totally burned out, suicidal, and on antidepressants. In her desperate pursuit for a touch from God, in October 2003, she had a Baptism of Love where God's liquid love totally transformed her life and transitioned her from being a Woman of God to a Little Girl with a Big Daddy!

Hindrances to the Secret Place—CD

He who dwells in the Secret Place of the Most High, will receive the Secrets of the Most High. As a Christian, do you desire to dwell in the Presence of God and receive the Secrets of the Kingdom as John the Beloved did? Do you find getting into that place challenging and difficult at times? In this message Leanne reveals what she feels is the main obstacle to our living a life of "dwelling" in the Secret Place. Find out how our true identity is the key to unlocking the door to the Chambers of our lover.

The Key of Favor—CD

Most of Father God's children have the Key of Favor in their hands, but do not know how to use it. It's time for His children to learn how to use their Key of Favor and unlock the door that stands before them, allowing them to step into their *Designed Destiny*. As you listen to this message, allow your faith to be stirred by the testimonies and prophetic activation Leanne uses.

A Marriage Behind Closed Doors—CD

Do you desire a strong and healthy marriage? After over 41 years of marriage, Leanne shares from her heart the principles that have contributed to having the great marriage she has today. Through this inspiring message you will laugh, weep, and be intrigued by the truths and realities we all face in our marriages. Whether you're presently married, looking forward to marriage, or know someone who needs a marriage like this, you will not be disappointed by "A Marriage Behind Closed Doors".

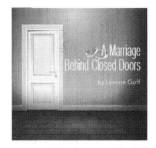

What Happens When You're Minding Your Own Business? – CD

In this message Leanne gives many biblical illustrations, as well as her own experiences, of what takes place when we are in alignment with the Kingdom of God and "suddenly" God intervenes with a new and incredible assignment that we were not expecting. Get ready! Just when you least expect it and you're "minding your own business", God's going to send you on an assignment that was not on your radar!

LGM INTERNATIONAL MISSION VISION TRIPS

LGM Mission Vision Trips are the experience of a lifetime.
The purpose of our International Mission Vision Trips is to proclaim the salvation of the Kingdom, the love of the Father, and demonstrate signs, wonders, and miracles to those desperately in need of a revelation of their identities as sons and daughters of God. LGM's Mission Vision Trips include such countries as:

Cuba

Philippines

Sri Lanka

Malaysia

S. Africa

Pakistan

And more!!!

Are YOU ready for a Kingdom Family adventure?

go to

http://www.leannegoffministries.org/vision-trips

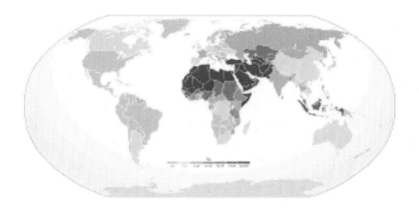

Made in the USA
Columbia, SC
18 March 2020